DATE DUE			

Juan de Mariana

Twayne's World Authors Series

Janet Pérez, *Texas Tech University*
Gerald Wade, *Vanderbilt University*

Editors of Spanish Literature

TWAS 654

JUAN de MARIANA
1536–1624
Frontispiece from George Cirot's
Études sur l'Historiographie espagnole:
Mariana historien.

Juan de Mariana

By Alan Soons

*State University of New York
at Buffalo*

Twayne Publishers • *Boston*

Juan de Mariana

Alan Soons

Copyright © 1982 by G.K. Hall & Company
Published by Twayne Publishers
A Division of G. K. Hall & Company
70 Lincoln Street
Boston, Massachusetts 02111

Printed on permanent/durable acid-free
paper and bound in The United States
of America.

Library of Congress Cataloging in Publication Data

Soons, Alan.
  Juan de Mariana.

  (Twayne's world authors series ; TWAS 654)
  Bibliography: p. 135
  Includes index.
  1. Mariana, Juan de, 1536–1624. I. Title.
II. Series.
BX4705.M3455S67   271'.53'024   81–13428
ISBN 0–8057–6497–6   AACR2

Contents

About the Author

Preface

Chronology

Chapter One
The Life and Times of Juan de Mariana   *1*

Chapter Two
Historiography: The *General History of Spain*   *23*

Chapter Three
Political Theory: Mariana on the King   *47*

Chapter Four
On Immortality and Other Topics   *70*

Chapter Five
Mariana's Style, Posterity, and Legend   *96*

Chapter Six
Conclusion   *108*

Notes and References   *112*

Selected Bibliography   *135*

Index   *140*

About the Author

Alan Soons was born in Grantham, England, in 1925 and educated at the universities of Sheffield and Nottingham (England), Zaragoza (Spain), and at Harvard. He has been a member of the faculty of the universities of St. Andrews (Scotland), the West Indies at Mona (Jamaica), Massachusetts at Amherst, and Rice, before joining that of the State University of New York at Buffalo in 1972. He was Visiting Fellow in 1980 at St. Catherine's College, Oxford University. Books published by him are *Ficción y comedia en el Siglo de Oro* (Madrid, 1967), *Haz y envés del cuento risible en el Siglo de Oro* (London, 1976) and *Alonso de Castillo Solórzano* (Boston: Twayne Publishers, 1978), besides several editions of texts and numerous articles and review-articles dealing with fictional and dramatic works of the Spanish Golden Age.

Preface

When Henry IV, King of France and Navarre, perished on May
14, 1610, after a thrust of the poniard of François Ravaillac, it was
immediately assumed that members of the Jesuit order must have
prompted, by their preaching or their writings, this horrible deed.
Of course, no member of the Society had ever promoted the idea
of regicide as a political course of action for Christians to consider,
but many had advocated tyrannicide, quite a different thing, when
oppression should become too intolerable. The most recent of these
had been Juan de Mariana, in his untranslated Latin work *On the
King and His Education* of 1599. He had indeed referred to the
slaughter of a king—whom he considered to have been a tyrant—
and had applauded the regicide's action. He had also brought up
some bizarre details in the matter of how a Christian patriot might
destroy a tyrant, but we are struck nowadays, as readers of the
twentieth century and with immediate historical experience of
tyrants, by Mariana's reasonableness and by his adherence to an age-
old tradition of thought previously illustrated by the medieval scho-
lastic philosophers.

In early seventeenth-century France, however, it was enough for
him to have been a Jesuit and a Spaniard; Mariana's work alone,
someone concluded, had lain at the elbow of Ravaillac. This is in
fact the resonance that Mariana's name has for the reader cursorily
informed—or informed in partisan fashion—about European politics in that age. Was not his book burned ceremonially in both
Paris and London? Then he must have been the quintessential equiv-
ocating and scheming Jesuit of legend. This book is written in the
hope of dispelling the irrelevant notoriety of Mariana and suggesting
his true claims to importance in the history of Spanish and European
culture.

There is no work in English on Juan de Mariana as a man of
letters. He has been studied frequently as a precursor of modern

economics in his *On Alterations in the Value of Currency* (1609) and as a political theorist in the treatise *On the King* mentioned above. This discussion of the author's work will therefore be concentrated on the works that bear evidence of the care of a stylist and a man of imagination, and his work on subjects ancillary to his two chief occupations, historiography and biblical erudition, will be only lightly touched upon.

Above all, Mariana can be illuminated as a representative man of his age—that of Fernando de Herrera, Alonso de Ercilla, Fray Luis de Granada, and Garcilaso de la Vega el Inca, rather than of Cervantes, Lope de Vega, Mateo Alemán, and Góngora—and of the Spanish geographical and axiological center. He completes the *dramatis personae* of his generation, but he is always distinctly backward-looking, to an older Spain and an older, sparer version of the Castilian language. This looseness of association between Mariana and his times has perhaps led to his being hailed at various times in subsequent history as a sympathetic thinker by the most varied kinds of publicist; his successors in the fields he chose to write in have faded as historical figures along with the values of absolutism which they promoted.

The writer must offer sincere gratitude for the generous assistance of many librarians, at the Biblioteca Nacional (Madrid), the Boston Public Library, the British Library (London), and university libraries at Harvard, Yale, the University of Massachusetts at Amherst, and the State University of New York at Buffalo.

Alan Soons

State University of New York at Buffalo

Chronology

1535–1536   Juan de Mariana born during the winter in Talavera, Central Spain, the son of Juan de Mariana, dean of the Collegiate Church there, and Bernaldina Rodríguez. Early in childhood he is removed to Puebla Nueva, not far away.

1554   Enters the Jesuit order at Alcalá de Henares and begins his novitiate at Simancas.

1561   Ordained into the priesthood in Rome and begins his teaching career at the Jesuit college there.

1565–1567   Teaches at the college in Loreto.

1567–1569   Teaches at colleges in Sicily, Messina, and Palermo.

1569   Removes to the Collège de Clermont in Paris for five years. The Third French War of Religion is in progress.

1572   Serious illnesses, "of the stone, the stomach and the head," afflict him. He is in Paris at the moment of the Massacre of St. Bartholomew. The Polyglot Bible is issued, containing evidence of Mariana's scriptural studies.

1574   Leaves France from Nantes, having previously possibly been on a visit to the Spanish Netherlands. Arrives in Toledo, which he never again leaves except for country excursions and his imprisonment in Madrid. He retires from teaching activities.

1576   In France, the League is formed in opposition to royal appeasement of the Huguenots.

1578   Birth of the future Philip III, for whom *On the King and His Education* is intended.

1579	Becomes an examiner for prospective clergy, and a counselor of the Inquisition.
1583	Date of extant letters from his mother and sister.
1586	Edits an *Index of Prohibited Books* for Cardinal Quiroga.
1588	Destruction of the Invincible Armada, which Mariana deems to be divine judgment on the licentiousness of princes.
1589	Henri III of France assassinated by Jacques Clément, and the Sorbonne absolves Catholics from any allegiance to his successor, Henri IV.
1591	Philip II reduces the dissidents of the kingdom of Aragon, and the "Justicia" Lanuza is executed.
1592	First twenty books of the Latin *History of the Matters of Spain* printed in Toledo.
1593	Henri IV enters the Catholic Church. The Barrière affair implicates the Jesuits in a suspected plot.
1594	The Chastel affair. A Jesuit eulogy of the assassin Clément is discovered.
1595	An enlarged edition of the Latin *History of the Matters of Spain* printed in Toledo.
1598	Death of Philip II and accession of Philip III.
1599	Publishes *On the King and His Education*. Assists in editing the works of St. Isidore of Seville.
1601	The Spanish *General History of Spain,* with continuations and modifications from the Latin version, printed in Toledo.
1603	The Jesuits are readmitted to France.
1605	Possibly composed his tract *On the Errors which Occur in the Administration of the Society of Jesus*.
1606	Final enlarged edition of the Spanish *General History of Spain* published at Frankfurt.

1609	Publishes his guide to *Weights and Measures,* and, in Cologne his *Seven Treatises,* including "Of Alterations in the Currency." He is denounced by Francisco de Acevedo and arrested. His tract on Jesuit errors is presumably found.
1610	Sentenced to prison in Madrid. Henri IV of France is assassinated by Ravaillac, and Mariana's *On the King* is banned and publicly burned.
1611	The Polish nobleman Jakub Sobieski visits Mariana in prison and reports on his health. Pedro Mantuano prints his hostile *Remarks on Father Mariana's History of Spain.* Mariana released later in the year.
1612	Publishes an edition of Lucas of Túy's tract against the Albigensian heretics, in Ingolstadt.
1616	Tomás Tamayo y Vargas prints his generous *Defense of Father Mariana's History of Spain.*
1618	Juan de Santa María prints a tract already advocating absolute monarchy for Spain.
1619	Mariana publishes his *Scholia to Both Testaments* with a dedication, to the later saint Robert Bellarmine, containing autobiographical reminiscences.
1621	Death of Philip III and accession of Philip IV.
1623	Philip IV confers the title of Royal Chronicler on Mariana.
1624	Mariana dies in Toledo, February 16, at the age of eighty-eight.
1625	French and Spanish versions of his tract on Jesuit errors appear in Bordeaux.

Chapter One

The Life and Times of Juan de Mariana

His Native City: Talavera

In former ages astrological belief, that the conjunctions of the heavenly bodies incline things below the stars toward certain destinies, did not only envisage individual human beings. Whole cities could also fall under some astral jurisdiction, and at the end of the sixteenth century two writers on the topic, Francisco de Soto and Frey Andrés de Torrejón, both explain that the city of Talavera, in the very heart of Spain, lies under the influence of the sign Gemini and the planet Mercury. This conjunction especially favors the begetting therein of men of letters.[1]

Talavera is an ancient city that had grown up at a point where the Tagus valley broadens out and where the shortest road over the passes of the Sierra de Gredos and the Sierra de Ávila comes down from the north. There are accessible outcrops of stone, which had made easy the task of throwing up fortifications at that point during the wars of the Reconquista. Our author himself gives a description of the layout of the city: it still has its citadel dating from the time of the wars of King Alfonso VII, though it has (1592) fallen into ruin. Around it are the ancient homes of the city's gentry as well as the large collegiate church of Santa María. The ancient walls of the city, with their seventeen defensive towers (*albarranas*) still exist, Mariana explains, but the city has outgrown these, and the marketplace and the homes of artisans and shopkeepers fill the space between these walls and some outer, smaller fortifications. Finally a circumvallation shuts in the city reaching to the river at each of its extremities; within this lie the market gardens.[2]

It had been long, however, since these warlike structures had been needed, and Talavera had achieved a total population of ten thousand or thereabouts, in spite of the incidence of epidemics, by the early sixteenth century.[3] No occupation is more dependent on periods of continuous peace than agriculture. Talavera lies in a very fertile region, a fact that is remarked on by geographers of the Roman Imperial, the Muslim, and the medieval centuries, and the most notable work on farm economics in Spain, Gabriel Alonso de Herrera's *Obra de agricultura* [On Agriculture, 1513], had been written by a Talavera farmer's son. A range of infertile hills that cross the plain were set with beehives; this may help to account for Mariana's notable interest in the names and the virtues of aromatic flowers.[4]

Early geographers usually try to characterize a city's population as well as describe its economic activites. Both Mariana and the later Francisco de Soto agree that Talaverans are indolent—but we shall return later to the fairly misanthropic temperament of Mariana. Soto says there are few heretics or persons lapsed into Judaism to record, and a number of ancient *hidalgo* families are powerful in the city. In fact, Talavera has a certain reputation for old-world elegance and a special attention to how good Castilian is spoken. He cites a gentlewoman of the place who has a kind of academy of stylish conversation and etiquette, attended by persons of quality from near and far.[5] Whether this early environment was directly conducive to the striking simplicity and propriety, almost unique in its age, of Mariana's prose style, is a thing we can only speculate on.

Our author was born in Talavera in the winter of 1535–36, the son of Juan Martínez de Mariana, dean of the Collegiate Church of Santa María, and of Bernaldina Rodríguez, also of Talavera and of obscure parentage. In early documents Mariana is described as *hijo natural* ("natural son") of the dean, and this has charitably been taken to mean that Juan was born before his father had taken holy orders. The phrase does frequently imply that a father was in a position to have married when a birth occurs.[6] We do not, however, know the relative ages of his brother and sister. The actual site of Mariana's birthplace is by now hard to identify, since Talavera suffered such destruction in the military operations that overwhelmed the city in July 1809. Almost immediately after he was born Juan was sent to the country and spent his childhood at the village of Puebla Nueva. To resume the question of the probable concubinage of Mariana's clerical father, we may observe that it was not unusual in the sixteenth century,[7] and had certainly not been unusual in Talavera. Who does not remember how the *Libro de buen amor*, [Book of Good Love, 1330 and 1343] of Juan Ruiz ends, with the laments of the clergy who must give up their ladies? Alfonso Martínez de Toledo, Archpriest of Talavera, for all his "reproof of mundane love" in his book of 1438, was himself caught up in a similar scandal.[8] The Jesuits, indeed, were to make the separation of clerics from concubines one of the principal aims of their internal Spanish missions. It is improbable that Mariana's own expressed sentiments against women reflect anything other than the policy of his society; we shall see that he maintained a correspondence with his mother and his sister.[9]

Down to the eighteenth century it was customary for historians, in their ignorance of the true circumstances of Mariana's parentage, to say that he "had a French mother" or was "of French extraction," and to imply that he was therefore no true Spanish patriot. These writers—Juan Hurtado de Mendoza and other chauvinists—might have reflected that papal decrees expressly forbade the appointment of foreigners to benefices, and certainly deaneries. It all appears to derive from Mariana's refusal, in his *General History of Spain*, to write a mere patriotic panegyric, and more specifically from his asserting, erroneously though in good faith, that Blanche, mother of St. Louis of France, was older, not younger, than Berengaria, mother of St. Ferdinand of Castile. Critic after critic brought this trivial datum up as proof of Mariana's disloyalty to Spain![10]

One small historical fact connected with the Collegiate Church of Santa María deserves mention, and that is the refusal of the dean and canons to provide funds for a bullfight during the festival of Las Mondas in 1515. All the secular authorities of Talavera immediately arranged to bestow rich endowments on the Collegiate Church—and presumably the irate population did not have to see its bullfight canceled.[11] The connection may be tenuous, but this small fact of history may have helped to confirm Mariana in his sour opinions on the subject of bullfighting.

It was very important for Mariana to be able to identify his native city with the Elbora of Roman Spain, rejecting the surely rather better claims of Évora in Portugal.[12] He would like, consequently, to connect his birthplace with that of the early Christian martyr St. Vincent. According to Mariana, the saint and his sisters escaped persecution at first by fleeing to the fastness of El Piélago, a hilly outcrop near Talavera, much beloved and described by him. For the conception of his works he needs a setting of great beauty, with woods and waters and the ruins of a church of the Knights Templar, so that they may grow "organically" and in sanctifying and propitious harmony with the legend of St. Vincent and his companions.[13]

Mariana at the University, in Italy and France

In 1554 Mariana entered the University of Alcalá, like Talavera in the territory of the immense diocese of the Primate of Spain, Toledo. It is possible that the academic career of our author owes much to the support of its archbishop at that time, the Talaveran Juan Martínez Guijeño (latinized as "Siliceus"), although it was normally the case that the University of Alcalá was in rebellion against the archbishop (Guijeño was, history records, a consistent hater of the Jesuits, so that Mariana would have immediately shaken off the patronage of Guijeño if it ever was accepted). He seems to have formed in earlier schooldays a friendship with another youth of Talavera who also later became archbishop, García de Loaisa. The two were students together, and Mariana later owed much to him in his career, so that some family connection between the two appears to be the decisive element.[14] We know nothing of his student career, and he next appears undergoing the Jesuit novitiate at Simancas. A Jesuit college at that time was a self-governing student corporation, so that Mariana's talents were recognized early and he began his teaching, of dogmatic theology, at an early age and well before ordination. From this period dates the anecdote, recounted by the chronicler of Talavera, Cosme Gómez Tejada, of the student finding no room in Mariana's lecture hall and perching at the window.

Mariana availed himself of the biblical quotation; "He who enters not by the door is a thief and a robber." To which the student replied: "In order, however, to steal your doctrine, sir."[15]

The moment came when Mariana's training required his removal to Rome, and it is pointed out that attempts were made to prevent this by the Spanish authorities, who were alarmed at the draining off of intellectuals into foreign countries by the Society.[16] Once in Rome, by September 1561, Mariana found that he had to change subjects, from dogmatic theology to biblical studies, and thus he found his area of permanent interest. He ever afterwards described himself as an exegete of both Testaments. We may be permitted to speculate, however, that this may have been a prudent move on someone's part, since much of the heavy censoring of Mariana's later treatises is directed precisely at correcting errors in dogmatic theology. Mariana's ordination followed in 1562 and his profession of the four vows of the Society in 1564. We hear of evaluations of his teaching, containing many complaints of his talking above the heads of the students.[17] Illness begins to be important in Mariana's life, possibly the malaria that oppressed Rome at that time, aggravated by the poor diet at the indigent Jesuit college and by overwork. For two years he was outside Rome, at the college in Loreto, once again teaching outside his true field: this time moral theology, for the training of confessors and assessors of cases of conscience.[18] His first substantive posts, at colleges in Sicily, Messina, and Palermo, yield us few historical facts about him, except that he was fond of insisting on very cheerful and spacious (*muy alegres y grandes*) teaching rooms. All in all, there seems to be little in Mariana's Italian experience that produces any resonance we might detect in his later works.

This is emphatically untrue of the years he spent in France, the next country that his college teaching career took him to, in 1569. When Mariana arrived in Paris the Third War of Religion was in progress between the Protestant Huguenots and the Catholic party dominated by the Queen-Mother Catherine de Médicis and the representatives of Spain. Our author must, we feel, have been incensed by the provisions extracted by the Huguenots at the Peace of Saint Germain en Laye in 1570: exercise of religion was permitted to Protestants with few hindrances, and designated places of safety were to be maintained for them as an armed force. During these turbulent years the most remarkable incident took place in Paris and was commented upon by Mariana; the Massacre of St. Bartholomew seems to have been regarded by him as somehow necessary, a kind of auto-da-fé without the ritual.[19] When he speaks, obscurely, of the innocents who were killed we may be sure he is not referring to the majority of the victims, the Huguenots. By 1574, the year he was destined to leave France, we may assume that he was entirely disenchanted by the Valois dynasty, observing the marriage of Marguerite de Valois to the Protestant Henry of Navarre, and Henry of Anjou, King of Poland, becoming Henry III of France, a bizarre but talented king, under whom civil war was to break out again, but also under whom the new party of neutral men of good will, the Politiques, was to make itself evident.

For the future author of *De rege et regis institutione* [Of the King and the Training of the King, 1599] the constitution and the affairs of France cannot but have been instructive. The French monarchy was totally unlike the traditional monarchies of the Spanish Peninsula. It was noticeably centralized and autocratic in complexion, above the law (*legibus solutus*), and with the capital city of Paris immediately under its control. With no concern for law or abstract justice, taxes such as the *taille* and *gabelle* could be assessed and levied at the king's whim, with no consultation of the Estates. During these very years of Mariana's stay two highly important political treatises appeared that aimed at a discussion of placing limits on this: Hotman's *Franco-Gallia* (1573), which insisted that a king of France should obey some fundamental law, and Beza's tract on resistance, to be exercised "by God and the Estates" in opposition to the excesses of any tyrant.

Apart from theories of state, Mariana would be very aware of the ascendancy and pretensions throughout all this period of the Protestant leader Coligny, and of the way in which his followers, though deprived of the central power, could permeate local governments in time of peace. Coligny had hoped to unify France under Charles IX against Spanish designs for expansion, but he had underestimated the sheer primitive force of Catholic feeling, especially in Paris, and the discipline and numbers of the Spanish forces. On both sides it became obvious that the great princely houses largely welcomed a state of war, in which their powers over both provinces and center could only grow stronger, while the minor nobility and gentry could be observed to live increasingly off war alone, without regard for ideals in the struggle. We shall see how Mariana's perceptions of such malfunction in an otherwise prosperous and invincible kingdom were to influence his political writings.

Mariana, at the Jesuit Collège de Clermont, taught at first as a substitute for the brilliant Maldonado, who fell ill at this time. He soon attained to the degree of doctor, either conferred by the university authorities of Paris, or by the Society, which acquired the right to confer it at this point in its history.[20] Mariana's illness began to recur, though we do not know what it really was. He prepared for retirement from teaching and the return to Spain, and it may well be that the sickness was a pretext taken advantage of at a moment when a consciousness of national difference was growing between French and foreign members of the Society on French soil.[21] Certainly Mariana enjoyed half a century of health, even in confinement, from this time onward. In his short verse "curriculum vitae" he says he left France broken by the climate and much work (*fractus caelo, multo atque labore*), while fifteen years later (1620) he changes it to merely much work (*multo labore*).[22]

The Jesuit Order in Mariana's Time

As a result of the political disasters in France during the early years of the seventeenth century the Society of Jesus occupied, rightly or wrongly, the center of every commentator's attention, and within the Society Mariana came to be the member most frequently blamed, almost certainly wrongly, for the turbulence culminating in the assassination of Henry IV. It is worthwhile, therefore, to examine the position and the nature of the Jesuit order at that period, and to decide whether Mariana was, in fact, a typical member of the order.

The Society of Jesus, founded by St. Ignatius de Loyola (1491–1556), and formally established with its unique constitution in 1540 by the papal bull *Regimini militantis ecclesiae,* bore many characteristics of an unmistakably Spanish institution. Spain was, after all, a country inured as no other to ecclesiastical discipline based upon vigilance, that of the Inquisition, which had been founded a good half-century before the Society, and the severity of which St. Ignatius had once had experienced. The incorporation into a new religious body expressly organized for militancy of many characteristics of the medieval monastic and teaching orders might have seemed anachronistic anywhere else but in a Spanish setting. This was the epoch in which even powerful and sagacious churchmen like Cardinals Caraffa, Contarini, Sadoleto, and Pole had expressed feelings verging on despair over the laxity and feebleness of much of the rest of Europe's monasticism. Spain's religious orders were relatively free of qualities that might detract from their purity of intentions and their vigor. Again, the sacramental attitude toward the military life, embodied in the institution of knighthood, was experiencing in St. Ignatius's day a resurgence (which some historians might, of course, call sentimental and vainglorious, little more than decorative) under the aegis of the new Burgundian dynasty, which now occupied the Spanish throne. This valuable vehicle of soldierly abnegation contributed much, thanks to the genius of Loyola, to the cohesion he envisaged as indispensable to the Society.

Spain had been the theater, of course, of the wars of the Reconquista, the slow recuperation by Christian men at arms of territories held by Muslims, a period of intermittent warfare lasting more than seven hundred years. Out of this experience, unknown by any other people of Europe on its own territory, certain indelible consequences emerged for Spanish culture: a sense of nationhood, to be distinguished from the sense of liege loyalty to the person of a monarch found elsewhere in Europe (and even in neighboring Portugal), which but for the accidents of later history might have crystallized into a state with its power vested in its citizenry;[23] and a realization that the endeavors of art, even those most appealing to the common people, may serve propagandistic purposes. One thinks here of the special additions made to the traditional ballad-corpus of Spain (*El Romancero*) at the instance of the Catholic Queen in her campaign against the kingdom of Granada. To the dismay of much of Europe, and that of members of many other orders even in Spain, reflections of all this were discernible in the constitution and the activities of the Society, which was also dedicated to a Reconquista, that of the realms lost to non-Catholics. Another tendency of the Society, unwelcome to many in Spain, was its eagerness to recruit members whose ancestry might not have been free of the admixture in past centuries, or even recent ones, of the stock of those who were not Christians at all, but Jews and Muslims.[24]

From outside, then, the Society struck the observer as most resembling a military body, with its general appointed for life, its principle of unquestioning obedience prevailing over private judgment, and its chain of command through provincials and rectors. Special abilities were sought in the Society's recruits, but imperceptibly special abilities began to develop in the men whom it attracted: a passion for reforming education, through the selection of an elite both in studies and in the sports of the age;[25] and a disposition to incline the policies of secular states toward the aims of the Society, by collaboration with rulers, not with the ruled or their assemblies. That figure of the age, the Jesuit confessor, began to be important (though rival orders still provided these), always counseling a certain "political realism" rather than kingly face-saving.

During Philip II's reign the Jesuits enjoyed no special favor in Spanish society or in the Spanish state. They concerned themselves on the whole with secondary education and with the first steps toward a superior intellectual tradition: restoring the quality of doctrinal and scriptural studies in schools of divinity, and ensuring that Latin language and literature were well learned in a country where such a discipline had been almost proverbially neglected. Only on a groundwork of elegant Latin could a philosophical tradition to sustain Jesuit apologetic against Protestantism be constructed, since Latin was the only language in which religious polemic could at that time be carried on. The literature of pagan Rome was impressed on the students in Jesuit establishments, not scorned as pre-Christian (the biblical parallel often cited by the Society was "the spoils of the Egyptians"), though this literature was usually selected either for its superior persuasiveness and hence its value in teaching rhetoric or for its power to furnish stirring examples of human effort, the great Greco-Roman demonstrators of Stoic *apatheia,* or heroic imperviousness to emotion, being singled out for imitation.

Mariana entered the Society by election at the very beginning of 1554, when St. Ignatius had only two more years to live. The "heroic first age" of the Jesuits was, then, just coming to an end. There were in 1556 nearly seven hundred members of the Society, of whom 140 were in Spain.[26] Our author seems to have flourished in the self-governing atmosphere of the Jesuit college, but also to have found the hierarchical politics of the Society itself to be a thing of no inspiring value. Certainly he sought no part in the government of the body, and as we shall see later, actually despaired of its ability to continue fomenting true apostolic selflessness. He was not in Rome at the moment of the completion of the magnificent Jesuit church there, the Gesù (1575, after seven years of construction and adornment), and we may infer that there was lacking in him the appreciation of quasi-theatrical magnificence, from that time to be associated with art commissioned by, or produced under the influence of, the Society. The Spanish Jesuits of the sixteenth century had not yet distinguished themselves as theologians,[27] though they did find a certain congenial niche within the world of divinity as ecclesiastical censors, after the publication in 1558 of the *Index expurgatorius* of the Inquisitor Valdés. This rather negative branch of religious activity gave Mariana his own first opportunity to publish his criticisms.

His notorious unpublished tract in Spanish, *On the Errors Incident to the Governance of the Society of Jesus,* was probably finished before 1606; he speaks of the royal residence still being at Valladolid. At his arrest in 1609 it was discovered among his papers, though it probably already existed in other copies. Mariana never retracted the allegations he made in it during his lifetime, even when the general of the Society, Vitelleschi, recommended this in 1621. Immediately after our author's death it appeared translated into French, Italian, and Latin, while the Society decided to proclaim it spurious, not by Mariana at all. It had its first Spanish edition only in 1768, one year after the disgrace of the Society and its expulsion from Spain by Charles III. It is, incidentally, a document that tends to reappear in print whenever the Jesuits are at odds with the state in any part of the world. There is, however, no English translation.

From what we know of Mariana's other, published, writings on governance the content of the work can be guessed at in advance: it enumerates what goes wrong with any organization, religious or secular, under an imperfect administration. "Parkinson's Law," the "Peter Principle," and other organizational maladies of our own age are adumbrated in the treatise, which has also a programmatic aim: to propose "cutting through the healthy flesh" before that which is infected slowly kills off the Society. It is not a particularly progressive plan, since it amounts to little more than assigning greater authority to the opinions of the Society's oldest members, including Mariana himself.

As a religious organization the Society had no models; that is the origin of much that has gone wrong, according to Mariana. The founder, St. Ignatius, could not have foreseen the eventualities that were to require legislation when he devised its constitution, any more than a father cuts out the clothes for all the stages of growth in his child when that child is born. A bewildering number of supplementary regulations have not helped, and the mission of the Society is being vitiated in all of its aspects. Study in the colleges is falling off; the faults are the perennial ones: a halfbaked innovation in material and a readiness to improvise, on the part of professors (which Philip II, Mariana says, had already had to stop personally among the Augustinians of El Escorial). The business management of many colleges has been neglected and several have gone under, but not because of a shortage of Jesuit regulations on fiscal and juridical minutiae. In other cases the fathers have become absorbed by their pursuits in farming and promoting trades, and the whole Society is being considered primarily to be a business operation by many laymen. On the other hand the novices are not getting their hands dirty, as future missionaries in regions of difficulty ought, and are housed as neophyte (and dangerously overfed) contemplatives. So the Society recruits more lay-brothers and dilutes its endeavors.

To the author of *On the King* it seemed obvious where to look for the origins of the disease: in the progressively monarchical cast that the governance of the Society had taken, and the falling away from Ignatius's trust in a representative assembly. The Society, like all other states, requires, that is, a mixed constitution. In the absence of consultation like this the positions of command beneath the general fall to schemers and ignoramuses, who can be very vindictive. Mariana cites the case of a rector of the Salamanca college who disciplined a member in a most unspiritual way, by putting into writing his doubts about the man's ancestry. He despairs of the general in Rome, a non-Spaniard and a bureaucrat, and fears that subsequent generals will have no familiarity with Spain or its mission field. Mariana's most powerful attack is on the infamous syndications, the system of personal delations within the Society. The reports from these never cease, but disappear into a secret archive for later use. The practice is palpably tyrannical: even pagan Roman emperors had executed delators; the early Christian Council of Elvira had anathematized them; the Society of Jesus, says Mariana, rewards them, and cites the harassment of the admirable Father José de Acosta, when the Society permitted practices that hoodlums (*rufianes*) could not have improved upon—and all because he had modestly proposed reviving the Ignatian General Congregation. Existing dossiers would, says our author, be better destroyed, since "there is no ointment to cure the wound made by a sycophant."

On the other hand, when the Society wishes to reward a member—which, Mariana concedes, might not occur in *someone's* ideal religious community; Ignatius, however, provided for it—learning, preaching, and literary excellence all are overlooked; the recognition all comes ad hoc and usually unaccountably in most members' opinion. There is at this point a curious distinction made between "arithmetical equality" and "geometrical equality" in rewards (and in other things), just as special shoes are made for special feet, not for all feet. It may be a first approach to the early Socialist "From each according to his ability; to each according to his needs."

Mariana admits that he is bitter, and he is willing to have his senility held responsible for it. It is at this point that he offers his scarcely acceptable argument that the claims of the older members of the Society ought always to receive prior consideration, even though their achievements may never have justified this. It is natural, given this direction of his thought, that Mariana should deplore the careers chosen by many younger priests as confessors to great personages. He associates this activity with any other kind of domestic, secular hanging-on in great houses, and biliously surmises that it is the grandees' thriftiness that ordains it: Jesuits come cheaper than chaplains with recent degrees in divinity from the best universities. He allows the incidental fact to emerge that the Dominicans in the earliest centuries of their existence as an order had discouraged the engaging in confessorship as a career by their friars, and the Society of Jesus ought to remember this. We may infer that this particular animadversion cannot have gone down well with Aliaga, the king's confessor who was to examine this treatise on its sequestration, and who was a Dominican.

The tract is in its way an illustration of how the doctrines of *On the King,* all of which were supported by good authority, might be applied to the immediate situation of the Society. In any century it provides timely reading for those who are concerned with the participation by the lower ranks in the direction of organizations. By the Society of Jesus itself it is still usually dismissed as an essay in utopian writing, with few historical underpinnings.[28]

When we have considered all of Mariana's life and writings we might arrive at a tentative estimate of his career as a Jesuit. It may be that this member of the Society, who was previously thought to be so typical of it by so many, really derived, curiously enough, very little from the *historically evolving* Society. It may also be true that *as a Jesuit* he gave very little to the Society.

Spain after Mariana's Return

Mariana returned to Spain in 1574. He had been absent from his native land for two of Christian Spain's greatest triumphs, the Battle of Lepanto, that great victory at sea against the Turks, and the defeat of the rebellion of the Moriscos in the Alpujarras mountains of southern Spain. These moments of glory, in which the king's half-brother Don Juan—whom Mariana tends to despise—was decisively in command, were to have no successors until our author's death. The wars continued in the Low Countries, and the inglorious acquisition of the kingdom of Portugal by Philip II was to take place shortly afterwards. Toledo, the city in which Mariana resided ever after, except for his months of imprisonment, which we shall study, still styled itself a royal capital, but kings seldom visited it. He made the Jesuit professed house in the now old-fashioned city his permanent dwelling-place, and was therefore obliged to undertake a few local pastoral duties, with the sick, with prisoners, and with children.[29] His career as a teacher of divinity was evidently abandoned at any higher level than this. From 1579 Mariana became an official examiner of candidates for the clergy of the diocese, and since he had the habit of using the reverse sides of letters for his notes many testimonials to the qualities of now unremembered prospective priests survive, often in illiterate and in at least one case in entirely phonetic Spanish. Others bear the signatures of important Toledans. Exercising his acumen in placating these powerful patrons while hoping to maintain the standard of the entrants to seminaries must have consumed much of Mariana's time, between assignments of censorship and the preparation of an edition of the works of St. Isidore, Bishop of Seville in Visigothic times, a task shared with others and under the patronage of the king himself.

A small light is thrown upon Mariana's intimate life at this time by the survival of some other letters among his scrap paper. First there is the Christmas letter of his mother, Bernaldina (1583), now a very old woman and helpless ("*no puedo menearme de un lugar*"). It concerns money, in the amount of 2,800 silver ducats, expected as coming on the high seas in the charge of a Segovian, for Francisco Núñez. Thirty ducats are for Bernaldina herself and ten or twenty for "the nun" (that is, Mariana's sister) to buy herself a new habit. But . . . the Segovian says he has left the money behind in Mexico, and Bernaldina hopes her son will help Núñez put pressure on the Segovian. There is also a letter from the sister, who styles herself Sor Catalina de Santa Ana, of the same date and on the same subject. She complains that the money, now stated as being 3,000 ducats, has been left behind in Panamá by the gentleman of the ship (*señor del navío*), and she is doubtful whether it will ever arrive. Her mother had hoped to buy grain with it.[30] The chance survival of these pathetic letters from home prompts us, perhaps, to a curious sense of their incongruity in view of what Mariana was to become. This Jesuit who was to be a subject of debate in the Curia of Rome and the courts of Europe was also the son of a woman who was distressed over a lack of grain for herself and her animals. A phrase in his mother's letter allows us to infer that he did occasionally travel back to visit in Talavera. Only one letter among these chance survivals concerns the family of Mariana: a certain Francisco de Madrid,[31] writing in 1594 from Talavera, says he has delivered some "crosses of Caravaca" to Sor Catalina, for her to make pious presents. There is no mention of Bernaldina, so we may assume that she died in the meantime, at an advanced age.

By this time our author was completing work on his Latin *Historia* and was embroiled in securing funds from the king in order to have it printed. These final years of Philip II's reign were not, however, propitious for authors seeking money from the treasury. The Invincible Armada had met with disaster in 1588, at great cost; there were military reverses, plagues, and famines, all leading those in charge of the Spanish treasury to engage in monetary imprudences, allowing the real value of the currency to fall. The scandalous debasement of coin that provoked Mariana to write a treatise on it was yet to come, but "bad money was driving out the good" (or at least, as we have seen in the Segovian's case, keeping it more safely in Mexico or Panamá). Mariana's letter to Philip II of June 1, 1596, points out that he now has his Spanish version of the *General History of Spain* translated and ready. (This need not mean that he personally translated it.) As was customary at that time the applicant suggests how the printing might be financed, and we hear that this could either be by way of prize money, derived from ships captured by Spain, or by customs levied on imports from England. The total requested is 12,000 ducats. The treasury official Esteban Ibarra laments that no prize vessels have been taken in recent months, and that trade with England is under an embargo. Mariana had to be content with only 500 ducats, granted by the Council of War, for his patriotic endeavors.[32]

And so the reign of the Prudent King, Philip II, came to an end. Mariana may have noted among its historical features the fixing of the royal capital and residence in Madrid, which meant the eclipse

of ecclesiastical Toledo[33] and the new feelings of apprehension on
the part of other regions of Spain, notably Aragon. He could have
observed Philip II settling down to be, above all other things, an
administrator, and allowing no interference, even in church matters,
from the Pope, while identifying his policies with the Pope's as he
understood these. A brilliant facade of appearances forthwith covered
a formidable machinery of bureaucracy, unfortunately corrupted by
the inevitable routine. The men subordinate to the king whom
Mariana would observe closest would be the royal secretaries, men
of great ability like Antonio Pérez (until 1579, and later on a traitor
and instrumental in Philip's destruction of the liberties of Aragon)
and Mateo Vázquez (until 1591), who coordinated the results of the
activities of the great councils of government (*Consejos*). Indeed, the
king envisaged in Mariana's *On the King and His Education* bears
many resemblances to Philip II in his successful years; the melan-
choly that tinges the historical reflections in "On Death and Immortality" probably is conditioned by thought of the misfortunes
of the final years of the reign.

The next king, Philip III, ostensibly the prince for whom *On the
King* had been written, lent his name to a reign which brought
miseries both to Spain and to our author. The successor to Philip
II soon allowed the state to be dominated by unscrupulous favorites
(*validos; privados*) such as Francisco de Sandoval y Rojas, Duke of
Lerma. The indolence and corruption of these men—and of the
scoundrels whom they protected, like Rodrigo Calderón—put a
strain on the machinery of administration and, worst of all, on the
currency. This was progressively debased by admixtures of base
metal; the resulting *vellón* became of problematical value, rendering
commerce scarcely possible.

Mariana had denounced this, using arguments that are those of
a sophisticated economist, in a chapter of *On the King*—a book that
owed its appearance, evidently, to the fortuitous circumstances of
the patronage and subsequent early death of Archbishop García de
Loaisa, and of the death of Philip II. The author does not mince
words concerning the devastation that princes make monetarily and
psychologically by their profligacy, and on his republication of the

chapter as a separate section of *Seven Treatises* (1609) and in a foreign country, Germany, the king's men resolved to silence him.

The signal was a letter of the Pope's to the *valido* Duke of Lerma expressing displeasure at the contents of *Seven Treatises*. Mariana was arrested and imprisoned in Madrid, although he was by now over seventy years old. He himself wrote to the Pope complaining that important people, for totally nonecclesiastical reasons, were holding up the sentencing; he hopes, moreover, that the Pope himself might pass sentence if it is agreed that he has in fact offended the Church by the circumstances or the contents of his publication.[34] The Spanish ambassador to the Holy See did not think it would be advisable to pass this request from the unfortunate Mariana on to the Pope, so that now the Jesuit had no defense against the vindictiveness of the royal confessor Aliaga, a Dominican who seemed to care little about possible doctrinal shortcomings in *Seven Treatises*, but a great deal about alleged lèse majesté. (Mariana had with his usual frankness written of "the profligacy of our princes.") Aliaga instructed the Bishop of the Canary Islands to try Mariana, though with a picked committee of four ecclesiastics "to assist him."[35] Late in 1610 Mariana received his sentence—though found innocent of any lèse majesté—and it included the removal of all ecclesiastical electoral privileges (these did not exist in the Society of Jesus); exile from Madrid (Mariana had always chosen to avoid Madrid); reclusion in a convent (he already lived in a Professed House); and the incineration of *Seven Treatises* in a special ceremony. Aliaga naturally considered this nominal sentence too light, and proposed another trial, by the Inquisition.[36] It is difficult to ascertain whether this second trial ever took place; if it did nothing came of it, but many commentators considered Mariana, at that time and later, as "a prisoner of the Inquisition." The Polish noble Jakub Sobieski was traveling in Spain and visited Mariana during his house arrest in Toledo between March and July 1611; he already attributes the punishment to the tract "On Alterations in the Currency" and speaks of it as inflicted by the Inquisition.[37] We do not know the date of Mariana's release, but a document of October 1611 informs us that prison had been discontinued for some time. It is curious to read that toward the end of Philip III's reign and when alarm was spreading in respect of the economic situation of Spain, ideas exactly like those of Mariana in the tract which brought him such discomfort appeared in the works of many projectors (*arbitristas*) and even in the *Consulta* issued by the Council of Castile in 1619.

Time (and to some extent the early death of King Philip III) avenged Mariana. The Jesuit authors were fond of Charles V's motto: "Time and I against any other two," and certainly this aged member of the Society could have rejoiced, if such had been his cast of mind, at the changes he now saw. The Duke of Lerma was dismissed and sent to his estates in 1618. His creature the impostor Rodrigo Calderón also fell, and in fact met death on the scaffold in 1621. Aliaga was packed off forever to a Dominican priory by the new king, Philip IV, and Acevedo, the first cleric to denounce Mariana, had to resume residence in his archiepiscopal see of Burgos.[38] More and more public men began to echo Mariana in their pronouncements on economic matters, and the new minister of Philip IV, the energetic and resourceful Count-Duke of Olivares, tended to heed the *arbitristas*, if not Mariana specifically, in his measures of government relating to recruitment of civil servants, agriculture, sumptuary laws, and taxation.

But our author had long before ceased to interest himself in these matters, and concentrated his last years upon finishing his biblical exegeses. During these years the octogenarian Mariana began to receive letters from younger men of letters, Francisco de Quevedo and, especially, Lope de Vega. The Jesuit cheerfully defended the latter author when he became the object of an attack, the details of which are obscure, by literary rivals. Lope de Vega in his turn honored him with the dedication of his *Triumph of the Faith in the Land of Japan* (1618). The tenor of another series of letters between Mariana and Lope de Vega is not so edifying, however. Lope was, of course, the secretary of the disreputable and profligate Duke of Sessa, and it is on Sessa's behalf that he writes to Mariana in 1620 asking: how ought a man of "my quality" behave if I achieve the favor of my prince? and, how should a magnate govern both himself and his estates and vassals, and also exercise justly both civil and ecclesiastical obligations? Lope directs these queries of his ambitious master to the author of the *General History* and *On the King,* showering him with flattering remarks about the (really very banal) aphorisms found in those works, and even about the works of exegesis. Mariana seems to have acted with laudable contempt for Sessa's impudence and (possible) thoughts of becoming a quasi-autonomous princeling of the German type.[39]

Even at his advanced age Mariana after 1620 was not free of worries about money, and we have a letter of his to the king alleging having had to borrow funds while waiting for recompense for his fourth Spanish edition of the *General History of Spain*. A thousand ducats were granted him, but they arrived in the spring of 1624; Mariana had already died, at the age of eighty-eight, on February 16.[40] Apparently he was buried in the chapel of San Eugenio, which served the Jesuit college of Toledo. When this chapel was demolished in the late nineteenth century Mariana's supposed remains were transferred to a new tomb in the parish church of San Juan Bautista, close to the Professed House of the Society.[41] In 1888 Mariana's native place Talavera witnessed the erection of a statue to him.

Character, and Some Opinions

Only one portrait of Mariana exists. It hangs in the Provincial Library of Toledo, has often been reproduced, and has a good chance of being authentic.[42] It seems to be of a much younger Mariana than the "Aged 88 years" inscribed on it would suggest; perhaps it is a mistake for "Died aged 88 years." All authorities agree that he was of diminutive stature; we might add him to the roll of the "great little men" of history. He also appears to have preserved many youthful physical characteristics well beyond his maturity, since Sobieski on his visit reports his having only a few white hairs, though he was at the time well over seventy and had suffered a winter's close detention.

The fairly conventional panegyric to him, conflated from the chroniclers Tamayo, Scoto, Andrade, and Alegambe (most of whom were Jesuits eager to emphasize qualities in their subject which would be of no detriment to the Society), prefaces Noguera's edition of Mariana's work: "He was of short stature, handsome of face, with a wide and serene brow; of elevated spirit, great heart and capacity for suffering; unvanquished upholder of the truth, of liberty and of true religion; chaste in his behavior and speech; modest, abstemious, taciturn; an enemy of idleness and scornful of dignities." The possession of all these admirable traits would, however, still allow for Mariana's having a formidable inurbanity, and not just for repelling gadflies like Pedro Mantuano, with whom we shall deal later. A letter written by him from Toledo as early as 1590 shows a distinct humorlessness. A correspondent had forgotten to prepay the postage on the letter of inquiry he had sent to Mariana. The reply is that he, Mariana, feels flattered that the post-carrier would accept it in that state; he has paid the bill with gladness at being remembered, and he would now like only to be left alone in his corner and henceforward undisturbed. He proceeds to ignore the query and signs the letter saying his memory is not so good.[43] In another letter, to the historian Bartolomé Leonardo de Argensola (1602), though he covers his statements with a Christian maxim—*"La caridad cristiana pide disimulemos unos con otros"* ["Christian charity asks that we not declare our true feelings one to another"]—there seems to hover a note of scorn also.[44] To an objection to some fact Argensola found in the *General History* Mariana responds that he does not want to engage in polemic at his age, especially when he, Argensola, shows such strength and erudition. Mariana makes one tiny citation, from St. Paul, whereas Argensola had larded his letter with dozens of pedantically cited authorities.

The insistence of the chroniclers of the Society on Mariana's heroically preserved chastity throughout his long career naturally provoked amused comment in the writings of those who were less reverent. The long article of the Protestant Pierre Bayle, which contributed so much toward a rational assessment of Mariana and his work all over Europe, as we shall later see, recounts an anecdote in one of his polemical "telling footnotes," reported from the Church historian Maimbourg: "[Mariana] lived nearly ninety years in the most meticulous cultivation of chastity, from which fact it perhaps resulted that his hands were as supple and flexible after death as if he had still been alive. I frankly avow that I do not see the connection between these two things. As to the question of a miracle, I do not know upon what analogy or upon what basis one might allow it to be argued; perhaps one ought to make use of an argument by antithesis."[45]

It is difficult to isolate instances of the personal opinions that Mariana held; his published works are crammed with the received doctrine of his age—or of a former age, one which the author would like to see resuscitated—so that it would be pointless to search for Mariana's own views amid the commonplaces of the rhetorician. His unpublished works, however, contain one example of the expression of his feelings on a sociopolitical topic, his fourteen-page *parecer* "The Origin of the Peasants They Call Old Christians," of unknown date.[46] Mariana begins by dividing the inhabitants of that part of Spain which endured the Reconquista into four social groups, according to ancestry: Christians who came from the north as conquerors; Christians who had lived under the Moorish states (Mozárabes); those who were neither conquerors nor conquered (essentially Jews and Muslims); and mixed populations. He proceeds to an assertion, perhaps impossible to substantiate, that the greater or lesser powers and dignities among the ranks of the nobility in those areas are due proportionately to the energies expended by conquering ancestors in regaining the land. Set over against these noble Christians in their exaltation (*sublimidad*) are the Mozárabes in their abjection (*baxeça*) and this social gap was the reason why the nobles felt no particular apprehension in history when these latter began to style themselves Old Christians.[47] Mariana is of the opinion that the occasion for this arose when statutes were promulgated, excluding New Christians—descendants of converts from Islam and Judaism—from the military orders, colleges, and church offices. In the absence of written records all the villeinage which claimed to be Christian is favored by oblivion and assumed to be Old Christian. Mariana compares this to the practice with regard to foundlings at church doors; these babies are always given the benefit of the doubt and become Old Christians!

When one takes into account the tone of so many texts of Mariana's time on the subject of the New Christians, our author's attitudes toward the Jews are almost charitable. "They had kept to their faithless Judaic way of thinking" (. . . *se havían en su judaica y pérfida opinión conservado*) is merely the routine rejection of Judaism as a creed by the Jesuit priest. He considers it hopeless to establish the racial origin of anyone not known to have ancestors who embraced Christianity no further back than the reign of the Catholic Monarchs. Yet, as he points out, to avoid daily vexations Jews and Moors became New Christians in all ages; even though they were only "low and base people" (*gente vil y baxa*, though Mariana is not implying here moral as against social "villainy") they wanted to till their lands, pay tribute to their eventual Christian conquerors, and live a quiet life. They had no natural inclination to rise in the world, achieved no fame, and their origins became lost in the "mist."

The longest section of this little treatise is distinctly more acrimonious. This concerns the descendants of the rebellious Goths who invited the Moors into Spain, paid taxes to them, and entered their armies against Christians from the north. During the Reconquista they behaved like the Greeks under Turkish rule, tending always to wait for eventualities. They never rose against the Muslims, either because these latter allowed them no weapons or because they lost spirit and reflected on what they had to lose. Even after their liberation by others, these Mozárabes and their descendants are base and infamous (*"Gente tan vil, infame y soez"; "gente villana y soez y sin nobleza"*). These are the Old Christian peasants! They were at all times a tiny minority among Jews and Muslims, so that the number of their descendants must be proportionately small, too; they are only Old Christians because we cannot, says Mariana, trace their true origins, and because we excuse their ignoble part in the Reconquista.

Our author is distinctly humane in this *parecer*. The worst moral vituperation falls not on the Jews,[48] and certainly not on converted Muslims or Moriscos, but on the Mozárabes among the peasantry. Had this piece ever been printed it could not but have stirred up even more enmity against its author and his lack of "patriotism."

Chapter Two
Historiography: The *General History of Spain*

There is a marked discrepancy in the attitudes of the Renaissance humanists toward history. On the one hand they held history, for the most part, in no especially high esteem.[1] One of the assertions they proclaimed most frequently was that they had superseded the works of their immediate past and had founded a new intellectual order. On the other hand, in their need to illustrate moral questions, they could not dispense with historical instances. So that historical knowledge was more typically passed on than taught by them as an academic discipline.[2] It was, therefore, usual for the historically minded humanist to value the anecdote or the telling action found among the records of the past as a means to awake the reader's or listener's attention during a discourse, at a moment when the mere iteration of the received truths of moral philosophy would only induce somnolence. Coluccio Salutati (1330–1406), with this in mind, had asked, *[Quis] titillante quasi quodam pruritu, ad idem audiendum non animetur?* ("Who will not feel himself stimulated to listen when he is being tickled as though by an itch?").[3] One result of this discrepancy is that there were few theoretical writings. At this time, however, the predominance of the extant works of Cicero over the schools of rhetoric led to a certain reverence for everything he ever discussed. In his major text *De oratore* [On the Orator] he utters his celebrated recommendation of historical knowledge to the apprentice rhetorician:

Historia vero testis temporum, lux veritatis, vita memoriae, magistra vitae, nuntia vetustatis, qua voce alia, nisi oratoris, immortalitati commendatur? (II.9.36)

(History is indeed the witness of the times, the light of truth, the vivifier of memory, the trainer in life, the herald of bygone ages. Whose voice better than that of the orator can lend her immortality?)

Furthermore, a story had survived of how Cicero had urged Livy to undertake to fill the vacuum where there should exist a great national history, comparable with what Greece already had.[4] Something like the interplay of these two movements of thought produced Renaissance historiography, dominated by the canons of the rhetoricians and by a nascent competitive nationalism, concentrated also exclusively on matters political, dynastic, and military.

Half a century before the appearance of Mariana's first Latin volume of history a Platonizing Spanish humanist, Sebastián Fox Morcillo in his *Artis historicae penus* [Contributions to the Art of History, Antwerp, 1557] had complained from his expatriated scholar's cell in Louvain that he could find no history of Spain of any value, and not even a panegyric to Spain's excellences more recent than St. Isidore's. He recommended the preparation of a Latin history that might make its way among foreign peoples with a message of Spain's ancient greatness. It ought, he said, to be written from no particular point of view, though even in such a work of vulgarization tales of portents and miracles should be left out.[5] Above all it should be ornate, ordered, and serious. Matters became more urgent after the defeat of the Armada, as the tendentious book of the French Huguenot Mayerne Turquet, *Histoire générale d'Espagne* (1587), began to acquire some currency wherever French could be understood.[6] It was an adaptation of the work of one of Mariana's predecessors, Esteban de Garibay, who wrote in Castilian.

For our author had some forerunners in the making of history who were far from negligible. In two cases it is an inescapable conclusion that they were Mariana's superiors in the craft, and even heralds of a new, more scientific approach to historiography. The earliest in date was Florián de Ocampo, whose first task had been to continue, within his lights, the ancient *Chronicle of Spain* first begun by the thirteenth-century King Alfonso X, the Wise (*Las cuatro partes enteras de la crónica de España,* Zamora, 1541). But he is more celebrated for a work of much greater compass, beginning with the creation of the world and crammed with "antiquities," fables of origins and bogus personages of his own invention.[7] This book, *Los cuatro libros primeros de la crónica general de España* (Zamora, 1543 and Medina del Campo, 1553), was to form the source-work of Mariana's earlier books, though the latter knew full well that any slipping from a judicious use of the work would be bound to draw criticism, and indeed it did. The next work of general history was that of the Basque Esteban de Garibay, which has been mentioned already: *Los cuarenta libros del compendio historial de las crónicas, y universal historia de todos los reinos de España* (Antwerp, 1571). Garibay had no easy command of Castilian, and also was possessed by an animus against the Roman Empire together with a fervent advocacy of the antiquity of the Basques. His book, then, is often quite untrustworthy, but his digesting of so many ancient chronicles in advance was extremely helpful to Mariana when the latter was approaching the medieval period of his own work. The work of Ambrosio de Morales, *La crónica general de España* (Alcalá de Henares, 1574–77), is quite different and approaches the scientific, while that of Jerónimo de Zurita, *Anales de la Corona de Aragón* (Zaragoza, 1562–80), covers a more restricted area of history, and is entirely critical and documented. All legends are recognized for what they are. The best elements of Mariana's work derive from what he learned from the last two predecessors he had.

The Publishing History and the Shape of the *General History of Spain*

Mariana may have begun to make notes toward composing his history as early as 1579, though this is an inference from the age of the letters the reverse sides of which he used; they may not have been recently received ones.[8] In any case by July 1586 the twenty-five books were ready for the printer, in the original Latin. Publication did not come, however, until 1592 and included only twenty books. This could have been a result of pressure from interested people retaining a sensitivity about comparatively recent events, or of a shortage of money to pay for more.[9] The work certainly proved difficult to sell; the *tasa,* or government revenue portion, was excessive, and it has been even calculated that a small vineyard could have been acquired at that time for the price of a copy.[10] There was a misjudgment of the public; few of Philip II's subjects read Latin with ease, while the elevated price and the omission of any statement of intended outreach to foreign lands in the original preface inhibited its exportation out of Spain. (The 1605 Mainz edition in Latin, of twenty-five books, was a better attempt, and did in fact reach a public of medievalists in Central Europe.)

Obviously a translation into Castilian was required, and this was done most probably with the help of collaborators whose work would be revised by Mariana. The year 1598 saw the volume, the contents of which halted at the reign of Ferdinand the Catholic, ready for printing. The preface explains the method, and the unsubservient attitude:

En la traducción no procedí como intérprete sino como autor, hasta trocar algún apellido y tal vez mudar opinión, que se tendrá por la nuestra la que en esta quinta impresión se hallare. Ni me até a las palabras ni a las cláusulas; quité y puse con libertad según me pareció más acertado, que unas cosas son a propósito para gente docta y otras para la vulgar. Darán gusto a los de nuestra nación a veces las de que los extranjeros harían poco caso. Cada ralea de gente tiene sus gustos, sus aficiones y sus juicios. En dar el don a particulares voy considerado y escaso, como lo fueron nuestros antepasados. Quien hallare alguno que le toque o se le deba sin él póngasele en su libro, que nadie le irá a la mano. Algunos vocablos antiguos se pegaron de las corónicas de España de que usamos. . . .

(In this translation I did not consider myself an interpreter but an author, occasionally changing a proper name and occasionally changing my mind. Let everything that is found in this fifth printing be considered my own. Nor did I follow literally the words and phrases in the Latin; I altered them as I saw fit, since some things have their place in a text for the learned and others in one for the general public. Some things please the Spanish reading public while foreigners may find the same things uninteresting. Every nation has its preferences, its enthusiasms and its criticisms. In calling individuals by the title Don I have been parsimonious just as our forefathers were. If anyone should find that he ought to have the title, or he has merited it, and it is missing, let him write it in his copy, for nobody will follow him up. Some antiquated words out of the Spanish chronicles I used have stuck themselves in the text. . . .)

As it happens the textual differences are small, and there is no special difference in approach to two publics; *romancistas,* as Mariana calls non-Latinists, are not treated as unlearned.[11] Complaints began to come in from outside Castile. Some Portuguese were incensed to read that after their great medieval victory over the Castilians at Aljubarrota there took place a national "bacchanal" (Mariana replaced this word by "with good reason" in later editions) and that there had occurred no miraculous apparition of the Portuguese religious emblem (*las Quinas de Portugal*) to their embattled first king Afonso Henriques. (Mariana called the legend "ridiculous," and then deleted it.) From Aragon came the letters of the worried Leonardo de Argensola brothers (1602) hoping that Mariana would change the reference to the birthplace of Prudentius from Calahorra to Zaragoza. Our author points out that even Gennadius's ancient *Life of Prudentius* does not say specifically where he was born, and proceeds to a private statement of principles, between historians:

. . . [yo] por lo menos suspendiera el juicio, como lo acostumbro en otros puntos controversos. . . . Porque como usted lo toca, y es así, yo nunca pretendí hacer Historia de Espana ni examinar todos los particulares, que fuera nunca acabar, sino poner en estilo y en lengua latina lo que otros tenían juntado, como materiales de la fábrica que pensaba levantar. Que si todo se cautelara sospecho que otros muchos centenares de años nos estuviéramos sin Historia latina que pudiera parecer entre las gentes.

(I at least should suspend my opinion, as I usually do in other controversial points. Because, since you touch upon it, and it is a fact, I never intended to write [the definitive] History of Spain nor examine every detail, a task impossible to accomplish, but rather put into stylish Latin what others had accumulated, this latter being the raw materials of the edifice I hoped to build. For if everything were caviled into I suspect that we should be as many more hundreds of years without a History of Spain in Latin which could be issued for all nations to read.)[12]

It was unfortunate, as we shall see, that Mariana had more surly and malevolent adversaries to satisfy than the two pedantic brothers in Aragon.

Obviously Mariana was caught here in the perpetual quandary of the historian: how ought he to select? Medieval historians had tended

not to select at all; selection was usually seen as the enemy of the
transmission of truth.[13] With the new prestige of Classical authors
at the Renaissance, however, the dictum of Cicero acquired more
cogency: the first law of history is that the historian should scrupulously avoid saying anything false; the second is that he should
be scrupulous about including all the truth.[14] Mariana evidently
had the enervating task of attempting to please everybody as he
decided how much he ought to include and how much he ought to
harmonize among the chaotic and contradictory sources he was han-
dling, in order to provide *enough of* the truth.

The history of medieval Spain is, of course, the history of the
several kingdoms. Garibay had in his work treated these piecemeal.[15]
On the other hand, Mariana adopts the method of the synchronized
narrative, not excluding prolix references to what may have been
happening abroad at any specific time. He never loses sight, however, of the primary unity of Spain in "prehistoric," Roman, and
Gothic times; and he pays no attention whatever to centrifugal forces
in Spanish history. The history of a particular kingdom, León,
Aragon, or Navarre, is delineated from the point of view of its
participation in the Reconquista; beyond its annexation to Castile
it is neglected.[16] This assists, and perhaps springs from, Mariana's
providentialist attitude toward Spain's destiny, its reunion as a state
after fragmentation as a consequence of the misbehavior of Rodrigo,
last of the Goths. The individual characteristics of each kingdom,
even the liberties of Aragon which he has so much praise for, are
only provisional and no longer figure in the account. This does not
make the *History* very easy to consult. Chapter headings tend to
exclude much of what really is contained in the chapter. ("The War
of Granada" is particularly hard to follow through the relevant
chapters), and an index is quite indispensable. An innovation, almost
certainly derived from Isidore, is the working in of ecclesiastical
history, Church councils, notable episcopates, and the like.[17]

Part of the charm of the work of a Renaissance historian, though
a source of irritation to the modern reader of history,[18] is the large
part allowed in the text to harangues and portraits. Zurita had, in
fact, been censured for omitting harangues at appropriate places,
so that the nonprofessional, ultimately rhetorical Mariana had every

reason to put them in.[19] We have therefore a large collection of discourses, including hortatory speeches to troops (often with almost
identical words) before engagements; long strings of commonplaces,
usually about prudence, attributed to historical princes and great
men (including Baucius Capetus—a personage entirely forged by
Ocampo—before the Punic attack); speeches and letters of reproach
of great ladies, including La Cava, Rodrigo's victim; and at least
one cliché from the pages of Livy—the frustration and shame of a
Capuan, Vibius Virrius, at the fall of his city—is transferred verbally
to a Moor witnessing the fall of Granada.[20] We are left with a
repertoire of model discourses rising out of, and reproducible in,
specific historical circumstances, that is, essentially a school exercise.

The literary portrait, accomplished with a minimum of actually
reported detail, had existed in the Castile of the fifteenth century
(López de Ayala, Pérez de Guzmán, Pulgar). Physical and moral
characteristics of the great are worked into an "ethopoeia," to fix
the great person who has seized the historian's imagination in the
reader's mind, too. Henry IV of Castile is, probably unjustly, fixed
for ever in this way (Book 22, chapter 15) and his successors Ferdinand and Isabel (Book 25, chapter 18). As with people, so with
cities: Lisbon, Granada, and Toledo merit twenty or thirty lines of
word-painting apiece; and so with battles, the phases of combat of
which are selected for delineation, not the ambient or the strategy
they may have formed part of.[21] Mariana has often been reproached
for his concentration on military matters rather than, say, diplomatic
ones. It is true that this penchant allows for the inclusion of historically unimportant battle scenes, but even more it allows him to
include a multitude of last-ditch speeches by generals and heroes.

If the verbal texture of these discourses and feigned letters were
of the quality of Mariana's prose in his shorter works, this would
be an achievement indeed, but the acuteness simply is lacking.[22]
Since he believes that humanity is by nature unchanging, he feels
he is justified in summing up an episode of history, or in prefacing
a whole era of history, with time-tested generalities.[23] But this may
be what has to happen when a historian is known to be working at

third hand. His readers will be looking to him for perspicacity, choice and judgment; the facts of history sink to being mere "illustration."[24]

"Tito Livio cristiano, luz de la historia de España" Lope de Vega (The Christian Livy, Luminary of the History of Spain)

The postmedieval discipline of history developed in the academies of the Italian humanists and at the courts of Italian princes. Many court historians were essentially praisers of the princely houses they knew and of the status quo in public affairs.[25] Yet with the inception of the dream of Antiquity associated with Petrarch in the fourteenth century there came about a desire on the part of many monarchs, and also nonmonarchical civic entities, to trace an ancestry from Roman times. This sent the court historians back to the records of ancient times, and of the newly dubbed "Dark Ages," to ascertain these origins, and in other writings than the pages of literature.[26] An example of such a researcher of origins in Spain would be Zurita, whose *Anales de la Corona de Aragón* is built upon original records preserved with respect to the former Aragonese-Catalan royal family. Parallel to this ultimately tendentious and submissive school of historians there was another group, not very numerous but also tendentious in its way, that of the historians of current events. The most distinguished of these is the bishop Paolo Giovio, who apparently saw it as his duty to alert Europe to the designs of Charles V and of the Spanish monarchy.[27]

The influence of Petrarch on education and morals produced the tendency to read historical works for the moral lessons they contained, not for any appreciation of a national destiny or of great men as national, as opposed to ethical, heroes. There was no teaching of history as a subject, as we understand that activity; it was always ancillary to the teaching of eloquence on edifying topics.[28] Historical writers became, therefore, although with the exception of the dynastic researchers already referred to, rhetoricians.[29] The historical writer of Antiquity whose works contained the most eloquence of the right kind was, in the eyes of humanists from Petrarch onward, of course, Livy. Aeneas Sylvius, Erasmus, and the Society itself, in its *Ratio studiorum* [Curriculum] of 1586, all specified the early immersion of schoolboys in the works of Livy, with their array of descriptive set-pieces and harangues by great personages inculcating the ancient Roman virtues.[30]

In the world of Renaissance politics Livy could be studied for possible application to both republican and monarchical solutions. His is a centralized history, omitting the history of the provinces, and closely concentrated upon political and military issues. This led to a contamination of historical writing by the advice-to-princes genre and the habit of political projecting. For this reason Vega, the Spanish translator of Livy (1520), dedicated his work to the youthful Charles V, recommending in particular its store of political maxims. This was, of course, strictly contemporary with Machiavelli's taking Livy as his text in the *Discorsi*.

Mariana's work seventy years later shows a remarkable likeness in its implications and in its method of composition to the work of his ancient precursor, who likewise had had no direct experience either of warfare or of politics. It seems that Livy had felt himself inspired by Cicero's complaint that a great national history was needed, one that would rival the endeavors of the great Greek historians. The resultant *Decades* is a work dependent upon earlier sources for its facts, for the layout and development of its matter, and for many points of interpretation, besides being "verbose and negligent" in its diction, according to the later Emperor Caius Caligula.[31] Livy's originality lies therefore in his rhetorical presentation of events and speeches and in his selection for emphasis of scenes of high drama illustrating magnanimity in action. Like Mariana, Livy stops short in the *Decades* well before his own times, even when we allow for the final books of the text being lost in the modern period.[32] Possibly this was to avoid controversial matters implicating the recently dead; possibly it was because of a prejudice in favor of more virtuous ages, as they might be discerned through a haze of bygone time.

Livy seems to have no conception of change and development in the Roman polity or in the Roman world outlook. From the beginning of his narrative Rome is ready-made and complete, it has been said.[33] His chief concern is then to show the testing of polity and world outlook, and the virtues, *fides; pudicitia; disciplina; pietas; moderatio* ("loyalty; modesty; discipline; loyalty to ancestors; absence of excess"), which subsume these.[34] In contrast to his source and mentor Polybius he is not so interested in showing an institution being tested, as he is an individual, a senator, or tribune, not the senate or the state.[35] For Livy the vices are continually waiting to ambush the great personages: *temeritas; libido; ferocia* ("recklessness; lasciviousness; savagery"). From the sum of all these characteristics of prominent Romans we derive in time by intuition a notion of what the Roman character was; it is not explained, but exemplified. When the vices take hold, moral decay is swift. For Livy it is a thing that comes from the outside, an infection from the Hellenistic East. Imported things and institutions degenerate in a new country, and that country is impaired by them. The earlier Romans had, therefore, the pristine virtues; their liberties were lost as imported fashions imposed themselves. When one adds to this the methodological habit in Livy of harmonizing all trustworthy sources the parallel with Mariana seems unmistakable.

Munárriz at the end of the eighteenth century was to identify the omissions in Mariana's *History*. He missed observations of cause and effect in human events, all of this being absorbed into the providentialist attitude; he missed the delineation of differences between regional and national human groups and the consequences of this; above all he missed the sheer conflictiveness of Spanish history:

. . . no se halla en fin el hilo que desde el primer paso vaya guiando por el tortuoso laberinto de un país, teatro de una guerra sangrienta y casi continua entre las pasiones más exaltadas y siempre superior a los pujantes embates de la ambición insolente y de la orgullosa y estúpida ignorancia.

(All in all he does not isolate the thread that might lead him from the very beginnings through the twisted labyrinth of Spain, the scene of a bloody and almost continual war which the most excitable passions wage upon each other, and always keeping its head above the powerful onslaughts of insolent ambition and of arrogant and stupid ignorance.)[36]

Like his ancient master Isidore of Seville, too, Mariana sees the Spanish Church as the repository of the mission of Rome. Only that the unifed state is now assimilated, after its long dynastic, piecemeal history, to the church in that mission.[37] This *General History,* in which the concept of the Spanish nation is first brought to light, or so it appears, contains therefore as by design a coalescence of civil and ecclesiastical histories.[38]

Facts and Fables in Mariana's *History*

With Mariana's name is usually remembered his phrase *Plura transcribo quam credo* ("I report more things than I actually believe to be true"). In spite of this being a remark made earlier by the Classical author Quintus Curtius, Mariana's reputation has become that of a purveyor of fables. This is, of course, exactly what happened to the reputation of Herodotus, "father of history, father of lies," merely because the ancient Greek author had tried to establish a distinction between what he considered to have actually happened and what he considered worth transmitting, even though dubiously true or even legendary. Everyone in any case concedes that historians always classify the facts of the past according to their religious or philosophical persuasions, and to test their beliefs against what they find in the record, so that the "general reason of things," in Sir Philip Sidney's words, prevails over the "particular truth of things,"[39] because that is what the reader of history goes to the pages of the historian for.

It is an inevitable ordeal of general historians of nations that their earliest chapters will fall victim to criticism of a hostile kind if not to derision. In 1643 Mézeray in his *Histoire de France* put the matter succinctly:

Voilà pourquoi quelques-uns de nos écrivains ne pouvant rencontrer des vérités bien assurés parmi de si épaisses ténèbres ni discerner des objets éloignés à perte de vue, ont fait du commencement de notre histoire un roman.

(That is why some of our writers, not being able to discover incontrovertible facts amid the dense obscurity nor to discern things clearly at such a great distance, have made a romance out of the earliest periods of our history.)[40]

The earliest medieval historians had generally cared about the reliability of their sources and the purity of the intentions of their authorities: Isidore, Orosius, Bede, and Sulpicius Severus may be cited as examples here of writers agreeing that it is better to be silent than to be a transmitter of untruth.[41] By the twelfth century, however, attitudes become less critical and less scientific. As history progressively became, as we have seen, a department of rhetoric, degeneration could be expected.[42] If a legend could teach a moral lesson better than an attested historical fact, then it were better to include it. We shall see one of Mariana's censors, Pedro de Valencia, advancing this proposition.

For an account of those early centuries of Spain's "prehistory" Mariana depended on his source, the work of Florián de Ocampo, which itself owed a great deal to the highly fictional *Commentaries* of Annius of Viterbo (Rome, 1498).[43] The primordial kings of Spain are prudently called "fabulous" by Mariana as he takes them over from Ocampo (among them is even ranked the ancient god Hercules), but the pseudohistory of Spain's Carthaginian period is taken over also.[44] It is true that we cannot say categorically that Ocampo's account is a tissue of lies, but until we discover a Punic or Latin source we have to conclude that it is Ocampo's invention.[45] Mariana is much more skeptical with regard to his sources in Garibay. The latter's Ibero-Basque "prehistorical chauvinism" is not to Mariana's taste (*Dicere non habemus; divinare non iuvat* {"We cannot speak with certainty; and guessing is unprofitable"}). He compares all native accounts of the origins of the kingdom of Navarre with mere "novels of chivalry."[46]

All in all, Mariana is very concerned not to be duped, and to keep himself aware of a public anxious to know the truth about events and personages in the past. It is of a piece with his concern in the related matter of holy relics: *Nos adoramus quod scimus* ("We adore only what we know for certain").[47] Yet this was the age of reaffirmation among Catholics in their veneration of relics, following upon the age of ridicule of such devotions by Calvin and others. In this matter, about which it was essential at that time that a clerical historian should have a definite opinion, Mariana did not yield to the superstitious crazes found among the multitudes. Indeed he was vehement about the contemporary importation of vast quantities of bones from the cemeteries of Rome. They could not all be the remains of the martyrs, he cried; many might be those of people who had been disreputable in life.[48] In spite of this the craze had to run its course; the multitude had such a desire to believe that it wished only to have the truth about relics covered up, not to have their authenticity dismissed as imaginary.[49]

This brings us to the part played by Mariana in the debate of the early years of the seventeenth century which concerned the leaden tablets of Granada and the accompanying "corroboratory evidence," the *falsos cronicones* (spurious Christian records). In this question also we meet with the identical twofold exigency on the part of the many, both clergy and laity, to have certainty about the objects of their devotion, and at the same time to have the inauthenticity of the evidence dissembled. The period of the pseudodiscoveries at Granada extended from 1588 until 1595. Relics preserved in leaden casings, with explanatory leaden tablets, were unearthed. On the plates were inscriptions claiming that the relics were those of Christians who had suffered under the Emperor Nero, among them being the bones of "Cecilius, Bishop of Granada." There were also booklets with leaden leaves inscribed in Arabic, also mentioning Cecilius as having been a converted Arab.[50] At about the same time a parchment with an Arabic commentary on a "prophecy of St. John" turned up; the prophecy is related by "St. Dionysius, Bishop of Athens," and is reported in Castilian by Cecilius. The Archbishop of Granada, Pedro Vaca de Castro, was highly impressed by these ecclesiastical antiquities, though from the very beginning anonymous protesters pointed out the ludicrous anachronisms: the impossible first-century Arabic (not to mention the first-century Castilian), even the name "Granada," which is not found in Antiquity.[51]

It was less easy for Mariana to be skeptical about a related forgery, a collection of chronicles published by the Toledan cleric Jerónimo Román de la Higuera in 1594. Román de la Higuera claimed he had received the *cronicones,* by Marcus Flavius Dexter, Maximus, and Eutrandus, from the monastic library at Fulda in Germany. At the same time he was preparing a history of the church at Toledo, and was inventing saints with which to dignify the ancient see. He found

the lives and miracles of these saints, of course, in the works of
Marcus Flavius Dexter and the rest. Previous minor church historians
had named these chroniclers; Román invented their "works." The
account of St. James's visit to Spain, incidentally, turns up in these
cronicones, and this was, as we shall see, to perplex Mariana and to
turn him toward a thorough investigation of the legend. As a patriotic Toledan it was hard for him to reject Román's impostures,
and he imprudently worked the information into his *History.*

Among the features of the *General History of Spain* that have
assured, or assured until the last century, the esteem of all kinds
of readers are its random touches of amenity, its fragments of erudition of a superstitious nature, not to mention Mariana's *obiter dicta*
on perennial enigmas of Spanish history.[52] Where there may have
been lively dispute concerning some question Mariana once again
chooses invariably to harmonize if he can, and if he cannot, to shrug
the thing off with a bald statement of the two positions.

It seems that every historian of the Renaissance felt a compulsion
to have his say on the question of Queen Brunhilda (Brunehaut) of
the Franks: was she a murderess or was she innocent? In the case
of the French contemporary historian Pasquier we see the obligation
clearly;[53] at least this lady, who died in 613, was a figure in his
own country's history, but in that of Mariana the disproportionately
long coverage she achieves (Book 5, chapter 10) is not easily expli-
cable. He defends her at length, acknowledging that his inspiration
comes from Boccaccio, *escritor de ingenio poético, pero de grande diligencia
y cuidado en rastrear la antigüedad* ("a writer whose genius was poetical,
but who was most diligent and judicious in investigating ancient
times"). Her case had in her own times had its European resonance,
and Pope Gregory I had written his opinions in a letter to her, but
the Spanish connection is quite obscure; we can only conjecture that
readers expected to see what any new historian had to offer, and that
Mariana complied with this expectation.

Mariana accepts the rehabilitation of Joan of Arc (Book 20, chapter
16) at her "second trial," and allows her the same praise as Jacques
Clément, "a perpetual honor to France." He is impartial over the
matter of the Knights Templar, though deferent to the view of their
innocence expressed by St. Antoninus. The fact that their adversary,

Philip IV of France, was also the Pope's enemy does not sway Mariana's opinion here, though the more than dubious evidence alleging the Templars' unnatural, sensual practices almost horrifies him out of his impartiality. The question of the Templars leads Mariana to a consideration of that of tyrannical kings being cited before the bar of Heaven: Philip IV himself, cited by Jacques de Molay, and Fernando IV of Castile, *el Emplazado,* cited by the Carvajal family. Here he is inclined, as a lifelong enemy of tyrants, to believe that the sudden deaths of these two monarchs so soon after the judicial murders they had carried out, were indeed God's judgments. A storm in Rome, which was totally unexpected but caused the roof to fall in on the heads of members of the Borgia court, was also one of God's warning acts (Book 27, chapter 7). Another way in which Divine Providence makes its dictates known in history is through men's destinies; Mariana is emphatic that the stars incline the extraordinary fates of men like Don Álvaro de Luna, "and everyone's nativity is of some moment" (Book 20, chapter 16). One may remark also the special destiny of the King of Portugal (Book 22, chapter 8). This affection for the doctrine of good and evil stars leads Mariana into the imprudence of including a purely fictional tale of star-crossed lovers, *La peña de los enamorados* [The Lovers' Rock, Book 19, chapter 12]; apparently he accepts it as true (to the jeers of his critics), only deploring the lovers' choice of suicide.[54]

A related theme in medieval history is, of course, that of celebrated prophecies concerning the destinies of kings. Merlin (whom Mariana calls English, and situates some four hundred years before his own times) apparently predicted the exact time of the violent death of Pedro the Cruel at Montiel (Book 17, chapter 13). The possibility that a hoaxer may have been at work crosses Mariana's mind; he could not have suspected his source, as modern historians do, of being pseudohistorical dynastic justification. The prophecy of the hermit Juan Sago relating to the death of the Grand Master of Alcántara at the hands of the Moors (Book 19, chapter 3) is treated less reverently; the mask of religion, says Mariana, will always impress the multitude and move it to irrationality. Juan Sago's vaticinations go the way of false relics and *cronicones;* the difficult thing is to decide where to stop in this process of demolition.[55]

Mariana, as we have said, permits himself some personal points of erudition to enliven his pages. The town of Sangüesa in Navarre was once called Suesa, and Mariana "suspects" this derives from the Latin word for "hogs"; at least Jaca—which is not so very far from Sangüesa—produces excellent pickled pork and hams (Book 2, chapter 18). The celebrated Bell of Belilla in Aragon has to receive attention in such a general history, since it has the reputation of ringing itself mysteriously as a portent of great happenings in Spain (Book 21, chapter 10); Mariana thinks there have been reputable witnesses and reporters of the phenomenon, so he refuses to dismiss it. Mysterious voices of armies in the night years after the Battle of the Catalaunian Fields in France (Book 5, chapter 3) are compared with the more recent ones audible near the Cape of Good Hope ever since the tragic shipwreck there of Manuel de Sousa. Finally he reports the irrational antipathy of Jean Jouvenel, Bishop of Beauvais, after the Hundred Years' War, to the red cross, since it had been the English device. He compares this with the mental phenomena perceptible by madmen and dreamers: things and people they loved or hated while sane or waking appear to be fearsome in their vividness (Book 18, chapter 16).

The Dispute with Pedro Mantuano

Mariana's age was, as we have seen, one in which the historian had reason to take account of a new awareness in the reading public in matters of religion and national (including genealogical) origins. The desire to believe, with certainty, went hand in hand with a new skepticism, and this was really no paradox. Our author, as we have also seen, had early encountered this section of the public in the persons of the brothers Leonardo de Argensola. He tried to gain their sympathy for his apparent precipitancy in research and composition, all in the interest of endowing Spain with a respectable *General History*. They fretted about his cursory overview, on occasion, of the original medieval authorities. Mariana gave them his patient reply:

> Verdad es que fueron personas doctas y diligentes, pero más ven dos ojos que uno, y a las veces los más modernos despertados por lo que otros dijeron miran las cosas con más cuidado y atención.

(It is true that they were learned and diligent people, but two eyes can see more than one, and sometimes more recent writers alert to what others have said can see things more objectively and carefully.)[56]

But in about this same year of 1602 another adversary of Mariana's method was beginning to make notes. This was Pedro Mantuano, a native of Málaga (c. 1585–1656), a young man with some training in divinity who had become librarian and secretary to the self-conscious grandee Don Juan Fernández de Velasco, Constable of Castile, later to become Governor of Milan. Mantuano was the first of many commentators to try to get notoriety by assailing some aspect of the *History*. An anonymous essay of criticism appeared first, in 1607, in which Mantuano explains that he is writing at his patron Velasco's direction. It is very probable that Velasco resented Mariana's superior erudition (even when he agrees with him), disliked his stand at the time on the St. James question, and even more his cavalier ways with references to the Velascos of olden times and to the nobility in general (and to their by now undeserved fiscal privileges in particular). Mantuano allows that Mariana is "prince of Castilian historians, without rival," but in such a context that it is clearly sarcasm.[57] Mariana at this point hoped to shake him off with an insulting set of hexameters (1608):

> Solivagum olim rudis aprum ridebat asellus.
> Ille premens iram et sedata fronte renidens:
> —Perge, inquit, nam te tua tutum ignavia praestat,
> Nec tu unquam tantis poteris me incessere probris,
> Tam vili ut digner generosum sanguine dentem;
> Nam quamvis noxam meritus dignusque malo tu es.
> Arguere et multis tua certe crimina possim
> Eluere et sordes quas impuro ore vomisti;
> Nostra indigna tamen sese huc demittere virtus.

(Once upon a time an uncouth ass laughed at the solitary wild boar. The latter, concealing his anger and showing a calm brow, said: "Go away, for your oafishness preserves your safety. Nor are your many insults able to hurt me so much that I should deign to stain my noble tooth with such vile blood, though you are deserving of my revenge and of coming to a bad end. To many I could point out your infamies, and then wash away the dirt which you have vomited from your unclean mouth. Our virtue, however, is unwilling to lower itself to this.")[58]

Mariana did, however, make a more civil reply (reported by Noguera, but apparently now lost). He defended the translation into Castilian once more, apportioned the blame for his errors to the source-works once more, and once more defended his inclusion of episodes showing the personages of history in an unfavorable light. Historians, he points out, are obliged to blame as well as to praise, otherwise their works cannot be a warning for incipient tyrants, parasitic favorites, and the like.[59] Finally, he does not approve of Mantuano's working like a hack, with other *consarcinatores*,[60] in the shadows and anonymously.

A reply by Mantuano (callng himself "Juan de Aragón") ensued, though once again the text has been lost. It seems, however, that this time specific inclusions by Mariana were ridiculed (for instance, the letter of La Cava, seduced by Rodrigo, to Count Julián, known to be a recent fictional piece) or else deplored (for instance, the suggestions that the female relatives of Henry IV of Castile were immoral women).[61] He also replied with an equal number of hexameters much kinder to Mariana. (Hippocrates, he says, once bungled an operation, but explained that at least a great mind was responsible. It is small minds which have no modesty.) Actually, Mariana had complied with most of Mantuano's suggestions in his 1608 edition, but the critic had not apparently looked before attacking a second time. To be fair on all sides, it was never easy in those times to be certain that printers had complied with stipulated correctional demands.[62]

By this time, of course, Mariana's troubles were beginning, and in 1610 the Dominican Fray Luis de Urreta took advantage of our author's sojourn in jail to attack him for irreverence. Mariana had rejected too many pious legends (St. Hermenegild's martyrdom, the apparition of St. George to the Aragonese forces during one of their battles, etc.).[63] Mantuano, *ese hombrecito* to Mariana, began to notice the competitors for notoriety and at last in 1611 published a book of criticisms under his own name, in Milan.[64] The substance of the book is as before, laden with sarcasm and feigned outraged modesty at the terms Mariana may have used, for example, to describe the vices of some medieval king. It was not so simple a task at this point for Mariana to satisfy Mantuano's cavilings. The censor of the new edition, Pedro de Valencia, was now insisting that Mantuano's complaints concerning the letter of La Cava and the "fabulous" Bernardo del Carpio ought to be disregarded, since these portions of the History, legendary though they may be in their entirety, carry important lessons for prospective debauchees and rebels. One sees how difficult it must have been to write history in that age of the hegemony of moralists and rhetoricians. For his part Mantuano wrote a letter to the king himself, adopting the same moral tone, and this time posing the question of what might happen if the matters recounted were taken as prescriptive of certain behavior, not as prohibitive. From the story (if it were true) of La Cava ladies will learn how to take revenge for outrages committed on them in royal apartments, and the state will be in danger. Princes will imitate Rodrigo, and present-day enemies of Spain might be invited in as invaders, or they may learn to be tempted to force ladies residing in grandees' palaces. Mantuano sees this as evidence of Mariana's misogyny. From the story (if it were true) of Bernardo del Carpio dissident subjects could learn the stratagem of making secret marriages with royal ladies. León was weakened by Bernardo's rebelliousness; Spain could be by his possible imitator. Mantuano proposes better models of conduct, which Mariana has not emphasized: the city of Saguntum and its suicidal defense; and . . . an array of four members of the clan of his patron, the Velascos! He concludes that if history books are to prefer fabulous heroes, why not put in Don Belianís and his peers among the characters in chivalresque fiction? Why not indeed include Don Quijote?[65]

To Mariana himself Mantuano seems to have sent an *Antirespuesta,* and also published it, but no copies have been seen since Noguera's day. Our historian was, by this time, beginning to tire of the controversy. Another twenty-year-old champion sprang to his defense instead. This was Tomás Tamayo de Vargas (1588/9–1641), who was at least his own man but in other respects just as much a pedant thirsty for fame as Mantuano. In 1616 he brought out his *Historia general de Mariana defendida contra Mantuano,* in which he jests at the inordinate growth of Mantuano's work from a slim pamphlet in 1607 through the Milan edition of 216 pages to a heavy tome of 322 pages.[66] He took good care to dedicate his book in advance to the Grand Inquisitor, Archbishop Sandoval y Rojas, but Mantuano sent out a shrill cry to the king that the sale of the work should be prevented, and copies should be recalled for censoring.[67] The Books Commission of Madrid had its own judge, the Licentiate Baltasar Gilimón de la Mota, and a lawsuit was instituted before him which lasted at least until the end of 1616.[68] Mantuano thinks that Tamayo has been most impudent in his rebuttal of criticisms of Mariana, which the latter fully deserves in any case. (The chauvinistic quiddity concerning the seniority of Doña Blanca and Doña Berenguela is trotted out as proof that Mariana has become subservient to things French after his stay in Paris; Henry IV of Castile has been unfairly represented, and in shockingly indecent terminology.)[69] Tamayo in his deposition before Gilimón draws attention to Mantuano's rude and unprofessional omission of Mariana's title of "Father," and then moves to the ad hominem assault.[70] Who is Mantuano? Was he not originally Pedro de Madrid of Málaga, who changed his name[71] (*Que él lo mudó viniendo en Castilla y lo demás que en Málaga se sabe y yo callo* ["Since he changed it when he came to Castile, and the rest of the matter which is well known in Málaga, but which I will be silent about."])[72] The obscure reference seems to be to the distinctly New Christian—in fact typically New Christian—look of the name Pedro de Madrid (while Tamayo vaunts his descent from ancient families of Ávila and Toledo). Nothing is made clear, since Gilimón may have been of doubtful ancestry, too. The outcome was that Tamayo's book was first denied to the trade, and then allowed to circulate by Gilimón after inspection. Mantuano claimed that the copy offered for inspection was not genuine, but at that point the documents in the case come to an end.

The tenacity of Mantuano seems to have had the reverse effect of what he hoped for.[73] Esteem for Mariana's work only grew the more, until by 1618 he was "the Christian Livy, luminary of Spanish history" for Lope de Vega.[74]

Historia magistra vitae: Mariana the Historian and the Political Writer

If Mariana had not proceeded to write his *On the King and His Education,* might it have been possible to construct a similar work from the narratives and commentary contained in his *General History?* When we scrutinize the *History* we do not find that this is the case very frequently. For Mariana, as for Machiavelli, Ferdinand the Catholic was the political exemplar of his time; his capacity for dissembling in a moment of adversity, with no fear of losing face, is commended (Book 24, chapter 16). In *On the King* one could hardly conceive of Mariana's actually prescribing such action. There are apparent contradictions, too, in the matters of John II's dismissal of his favorite Don Álvaro de Luna and of the public deposition of Henry IV of Castile.[75] To be consistent Mariana should have applauded these political actions; instead he uses them for moral lessons on turpitude in high places and for a meditation on the occult powers of the stars over great personages. The politics of "realism" is also moralized; Mariana allows a "right" to Navarre to Ferdinand, citing the biblical sentence of Ecclesiasticus 8:8—*Regnum a gente in gentem transfertur propter iniustitias et iniurias et contumelias et diversos dolos* ("Kingdoms pass from nation to nation through injustices, iniquities, insolences and many kinds of chicanery")—as though it were prescriptive. Naked power as the final resource of kings is excuse enough for Philip II's arrogation to himself of a "right" to Portugal. (This last instance occurs in the Summary of 1619.)[76]

From Petrarch onward the historical writings of the Italian humanists had moved from being records of divine handiwork to being studies of how men handled their own political fates. This historical tradition culminated in the great early sixteenth-century history of Guicciardini, the conveyor of dispassionate political intelligence.[77] This manifests itself in the speeches reported by him; the hidden thought of the speaker is revealed in dialogue; politics is viewed as concrete and from the inside of continuing controversies.[78] Mariana seems to be unaware of this approach, or he is antipathetic to it. Political process interests him, but only for its outcome;[79] the dialogue attributed to his political figures amounts to little more than

series of commonplaces about prudence, tending moreover to echo
the author's own moralizings outside the narrative. The tenor of the
events narrated leaves a resonance in the mind of the *General History*
not of true politics so much as combativeness, military rather than
civil history. This is the result of Mariana's lack of interest in
recording the fortunes of laws and institutions, except insofar as
they help to illustrate the centripetal forces in the Peninsula that
he wishes to present as perpetually at work. Except for the office
of Justicia in Aragón and the municipal activity in Pamplona, the
only institution he spends much time studying is the monarchy at
the center. This may be, of course, a reflection of Mariana's perception of the crisis of that monarchy in his day. What historians
want their readers to be aware of in their political past, it has been
said, is governed by social movements in those historians' own day.[80]
The *Historia general* might then be viewed as prescriptive of a shoring
up of the centralizing monarchy.

The awareness of the multifarious crisis at the Spanish center and
the prevalence of political cabals in high places led slowly to a
substitution of Livy as the model historian by Tacitus.[81] The writing
of history to substantiate or frame political maxims became the
fashion;[82] Mariana's type of long, moralized accumulation of narratives around a theme of providential mission passed from the
Spanish historiographical scene, except of course for those who
merely required a book about Spain's past, the national glories and
disasters; for them, the politically unconcerned, Mariana's great
work and its subsequent continuations were always there.

Concluding Reflections on the *General History*

Mariana was aware, as we have seen, that history is a study of
process; he differed from many other historians of his times in a
dogged tenacity to the idea of providential guidance of that process.
For him the past and the present were unmediated theaters of God's
judgments. He could not, of course, be aware that it was his own
imagination, conditioned by his specialized moral training and conscious intention, which was singling out the superior men in history
whom he allotted the most space to,[83] and the notable events he

sought to place in the foreground. The unlucky in history, it has been remarked, are also the unlucky in historiography;[84] Mariana made no attempt to go beyond the partiality of sources that might have stigmatized such unlucky personages. King Pedro the Cruel (as he is in Ayala's partisan *Chronicle*) prevails over King Pedro the Justiciar (as he is in chronicles Mariana did not know of or happen to use).

Our historian seems to have no sense of vocation to be a historian of enigmas, of inexplicable events.[85] The current of time is, of course, dotted with particulars, and not with wholly rational phenomena proceeding from wholly traceable causes.[86] The philosophical grounding of Mariana's historiography was the study of universals;[87] the inexplicable had to be either distorted (by intruding some conceivable reference to divine wrath, perhaps) or to be shrugged off. We so often observe Mariana doing this.[88] Another inhibition enforced by this philosophy of universals is that against characterizing the Spanish tradition (*la hispanidad*) as in any way unique. But it has been acutely noted that the men who would seek to know most from history, and not to repeat mistakes out of an ignorance of history, would be the jurist and the ruler.[89] These men had to live and act in a secular world, confronted continually by unique events thrown before them by Fortune, and among unique institutional traditions, the results of the enigmatic workings of immemorial Custom.[90] A historian such as Mariana was unequipped to assist these directors of the destinies of men, with his moralized narratives.[91]

Besides the writers of general histories another historiographical group was at work. These were the specialized historians of dynasties, of juridical institutions, of ecclesiastical foundations, of universities and others, all absolved from so close a dependence on narrative as the basis of their work.[92] These are the true antecedents of the social philosopher of history, such as Giambattista Vico, and of the historicists of the nineteenth century.[93] Mariana, then, may be said to be writing within a tradition on its way to extinction. He recognized, obscurely, that writing history is providing a social instrument for rulers in an age, but he could not conceive of history operating in this way when every aspect of society would be eventually secular-

ized, history as the patient distillation of documentary records left
by institutions and not as the incessant inference of divine pleasure
and divine wrath.

La grandeza de España conservará esta obra, que a las veces hace estimar
y durable la escritura el sujeto de que trata ("The grandeur of Spain will
preserve this work, for sometimes the written text achieves veneration and durability through the subject it treats of"). This Mariana
had predicted in his preface, though we might feel the temptation
to reverse the terms of what he says. Though Mantuano, the Marquis
of Mondéjar (1628–1708), and Munárriz all quarreled with the
"treatment of the subject" in years to come (and Fueter in our own
century), the "written text," like a historian's Escorial, came to be
consubstantial with whatever grandeur Spanish history could be said
to have had.

Chapter Three

Political Theory: Mariana on the King

At some time before 1585 the preceptor of the young heir to the throne, Philip—and also Mariana's ecclesiastical friend—García de Loaisa, had recommended the writing of a treatise which would combine moral philosophy and deductions from history, as an aid in the training of the prince.[1] Our author very probably began work on it immediately, but it cannot be too strongly emphasized that he was at the same time engaged in a long and laborious task of editing works by Isidore, Bishop of Seville in Visigothic times (c. 560–636). Two spurious derivations of names for kings in the bishop's celebrated compendium *The Etymologies:* "reges *a recte agendo*" ("Kings derive their name from doing right") and "basileis *vocantur quod . . . bases populum sustinent. Unde et bases coronas habent*" ("Kings are so called because they are the bases which hold up the people. That is why [an architect's] bases have crowns")[2] can be perhaps discerned as propositions that Mariana finally wishes to substantiate in his *On the King and His Education.* His expressed concern, given in his preface addressed to the prince, is merely to confirm what he has undoubtedly already learned from court philosophers and from the king his father.

The tripartite treatise is provided with a setting of great beauty. This is the rural retreat of El Piélago, close to Talavera, a fastness shut in from the fertile plain, with a cavern reputed to have been a refuge for the Early Christian martyrs St. Vincent and his sisters. Also at the site there is a ruin, possibly of a commandery of the Knights Templar in more ancient times,[3] now surrounded by a pleasant garden and orchard and crumbling amid many springs and brooks which, Mariana believes, gave the place its name of El

Piélago. At this rural retreat Canon Juan Calderón of Toledo is recovering from an illness. He invites Mariana there in the summer of 1590, and also another clerical associate, Father Suasola, a true Basque *(verdadero cántabro)*. The outlook from El Piélago, over lands of the Loaisas, turns the conversation toward Mariana's friend and his commission of years before, the handbook for a ruler destined for the Infante Philip.

Mariana begins his treatise with a magnificent chapter on the origins of human society, and the forces inherent in it from the beginning that produced the kingly office. Primitive man was, for our author, determined by his weakness; man is born fragile and naked, totally helpless. This truth has led to the invention of every social and religious institution we have. There is no insistence on the biblical account of man's origins at all; from Mariana's text we may only infer that he "came from nowhere," and that his uncomfortable life in the earliest ages was by no means the result of any Fall from Grace. Families appear, and later larger agglomerations of people; we have society in its raw state *(quandam populi formam rudem)*, but its endeavors are already essentially cooperative. This is a Golden Age, described in terms taken from Virgil (and not so very different ones from those of Don Quijote in his speech to the Goatherds).[4] It is a time of fraternity and equality, without assertiveness, mendacity, or violence. But God himself has made man desirous of more in life, and even amid so placid and sensible a society there comes about a preponderance of the strong over the simple and the innocent. It is true that Mariana is none too clear about how this happened; he still refuses to advance any religious explanation in his text.

Man's weakness, as we have noticed Mariana saying, obliges him to be a social being, and at the same time a rational being. Given the disparities in human society between its members, men will tend imperceptibly to assemble themselves around, and to yield powers to, the wisest and the most authoritative in moral questions; monarchy has indeed, in this view, as ancient an origin as social living itself. He makes no mention specifically of a compact, and seems more concerned to demonstrate the antiquity of the state, of authority, than that of civic responsibilities and freedoms.[5] He does insist, however, that in primordial ages the kingly office was elective rather than hereditary. It is noticeable that Mariana omits any consideration of the divinity of regal institutions at their beginning; they are divine only at a remove, since human reason acting with divine inspiration really invented them.[6]

The advancement of societies and the patent wickedness of many men brought about the necessity for written laws, again of divine inspiration and cognate with the Natural Law of what is basically just and what is unjust.[7] Kings became lawgivers, and also prudently placed themselves beneath the laws. But ambitious men—Ninus, Cyrus, Alexander, Caesar—engrossed their dominions at the expense of smaller kings and governed vast territories personally; these were the first tyrants. Mariana concedes that most monarchies of his own times, even when not tyrannous, cover large territories once annexed by tyrants.

This brings him to the monarchies of his own day, and to their possible future. Monarchy assures stability when other types of government prove to be too easily removed. A king can stand above party and can assure civic peace as an arbiter. Prosperity, glory, and peace can attach themselves uniquely to the person, the lineage, and the reign of a monarch. The question of succession imposes itself immediately, in view of the actual horrors attending many interregna throughout history. Mariana discusses this very patiently, conceding that election has often procured good replacements for bad kings, and also that whole dynasties seem to have fallen into degeneration, notably the Trastamaras of Castile. The process of election, however, will always be prejudicial to the monarch later in his reign, while no subject will have doubts about a monarch who has succeeded dynastically. The hereditary king, moreover, will be careful to pass on a flourishing kingdom to his descendants, and will also take care to train his descendants in advance for their responsibility. And as the whole treatise suggests, the craft of kingship is best learned at an early age. The king ought to have the right to pass over an older son, provided that the assembly of his subjects approves of this— Mariana instances the disinherited, and at that time already dead, brother of the prince he is addressing, the notorious Don Carlos (1545–68). He is surprisingly favorable to the concept of female succession, finding precedents in both ancient Hebrew and ancient Basque traditions; and he could have cited—but does not—the successful reign of the prince's great-great-grandmother Queen Isabel.

Mariana at this point considers the serious objections of other theorists who have favored absolute monarchy. If the king's sovereignty is limited and if there is in the kingdom no appeal to the justice of the monarch as superior, then the state is no real monarchy at all, but a popular republic with a figurehead. Our author concedes this, but points out that in Spain at least the founders of lines of kings have always been chosen by examination by their subjects and subsequent popular acclaim. The sovereignty of kings resides for Mariana in the duties that the representatives of the orders of the people have laid upon them: of being a superior leader in war and an effective lawgiver in peace, above all of being a trustworthy levier of taxes to which they have consented. Since 1600, of course, these responsibilities of monarchs are yielding more and more to royal desires for power at the expense of their peoples. Mariana realizes this, and regrets the impossibility of reviving in his age the ancient liberties of subjects. As a theorist, however, he recommends the constitution of a body of superior subjects who would have the task of reining in the will of the king; he argues for the value in their times of the Ephoroi of ancient Sparta. He brings forward a modern instance, the Justicia Mayor of Aragón, who had precisely this restraining power. (He speaks of that office as subsisting, but the last Justicia, Lanuza, was to suffer execution in 1591 by what could be considered an act of tyranny on Philip II's part.) In latter days, Mariana believes, no group of men has qualified itself better for this function than the episcopate.[8] This may appear to be a kind of clerical absolutism, but no alternative group can be discerned, only the hateful court favorites, who bid fair to bring about the decay of both state *and* church.

This disaster affecting states and churches in many parts of Europe in the sixteenth century—rebellions, civil wars, schisms, and real or pretended reformations—is, according to Mariana, largely the handiwork of ambitious lay magnates and others who have abetted the greed and cruelty of kings. Bishops, provided of course that

they are not the same magnates and schemers elevated to the episcopate by kings, can correct this tendency, give an example to all
men in office by their exemplary lives, and in their celibate state
and elected status not inflict on the republic any line of greedy
descendants. On their position of strength within the kingdom will
rest the strength of the kingdom. For this reason, if for no reason
of conscience, the king must never deprive the Church of freedom
of action by appropriating its gold or its estates. Ancient kings of
Castile did this and their land suffered mishaps in the contest with
Islam; King Ferdinand scrupulously denied himself the expropria-
tion of church revenues and enjoyed a glorious reign. This may
appear to us to be coincidence, but Mariana's providentialist views
do not admit of coincidences in such a domain.

The prince is constrained at all times by the laws: divine law
governing his moral actions as a man; the rules of custom controlling
his reputation and his "image";[9] and the human legal code founded
on the sagacity of his subjects. He may initiate legislation, but only
at moments of great urgency in the state, and then in the name of
the commonwealth. He must be seen to obey these laws, and may
only proceed to amend the important ones—on succession, taxation,
and religious policy—with the unanimous support of his subjects.
The notion of *rex legibus solutus,* sometimes roughly rendered in
English as "The king can do no wrong" (and which survived in
ghostly fashion in Great Britain, for instance, as a residue of Divine
Right until the twentieth century) is rejected root and branch by
Mariana. He seems to have been careful not to have allowed the
reader the impression that the alternative to this constitutional
monarch, hedged around with juridical obstructions to his will,
would be a tyrant. The atrocities of tyranny have already all been
introduced further back in the treatise, and this is no doubt Mariana's
intentional layout of his material;[10] possible opponents of this limitation (and he concedes that these number among them many men
of respectable erudition) are given cause for reflection on tyranny
first, and only after the chapters on religion does Mariana essay his
scheme of constitutionalism.

The reader should not expect any novelty in Mariana's response
to his own question, "Is it legitimate to kill a tyrant?" It is a rare

political theorist in any age who has had any doubt, and it is a rare man of letters who has not counted as noble any true successor of Harmodius, Aristogiton, and Brutus, since these men were virtuous and risked their own lives. The case of the tyrant who has obtained his power legitimately and has then shown his true colors, or degenerated, or adopted—like the example Mariana concentrates upon, Henry III of France—the cause and the methods of a criminal party, is rather different. If there is any possibility, or time to act, his removal by murder ought to be voted upon by an assembly. The act ought to be compatible with public ideas of heroism, though tyrants can frequently only be struck down by secret means. Mariana makes his notorious distinction between poison in a drink (of which he irrationally disapproves) and that allowed to impregnate a garment or a saddle (which he thinks less objectionable, and as having been effective when used against petty tyrants in Spain's Moorish past). He offers us Jacques Clément, who risked his life after consulting religious authorities about his project, as a praiseworthy tyrannicide. We might not ourselves approve of the wielder of a *poisoned* weapon, as Jacques Clément was.

The second section of Mariana's treatise, on the process of educating a future ruler, has no special originality. It recommends a humanistic training, one which could have come from the pen of Erasmus or Luis Vives in the previous century. A model used by Mariana is, obviously, the *Institutio* of Erasmus, written for the young prince's grandfather Charles V.[11] The curriculum, in the widest sense, that is sketched out, from breastfeeding by the actual mother of the prince,[12] through his eventual cultivation of Latin as a spoken language and as a medium of all valuable literature, to keeping faith at all times and maintaining only honorable companionships, is entirely comparable with all others of the age, a more prolix version of Polonius's counsels to Laertes. We may only remark the relatively long and patient section that Mariana devotes to the prince's acquisition of a taste for music, for both its relaxing and its metaphysically suggestive qualities.

The third portion of the treatise deals with public administration and the recruitment of the men who are to be the supports of the state. As one might expect in Mariana, careers ought to be open to talent alone, and no man should in principle hold a plurality of offices. A system of inspection can do more for the administration than overprecise rules about the duration of powers and such. This is an obvious position for Mariana to take, since he has in mind in so many cases the conferring of these powers on prelates of the Church, a salutary contamination of temporal by spiritual power. One important caveat is that bishoprics should not for this reason be bestowed on personages belonging to politically powerful families; the reverse movement is the beneficial one. And among bishops those most suited to political leadership are the theologians, who understand the ramifications of heresy into politics, not the canon lawyers.

He passes then to the minor posts in government. He does not exactly exclude the ancient or the recent nobility, but recognizes no particular merit in its lineages. Much more to be preferred are the rich, since their holding office will allow the state to profit from their wealth and from their apprehensiveness because of it. Mariana follows the doctrine of Furió Ceriol in advocating a sharing out of offices among all nationalities living within the Monarchy: Castilians, but also Belgians, Italians, Catalans, Sicilians, and the rest.[13] The strength of the Monarchy for Mariana, as in his time for Erasmus, lay in its sturdy local features, not in its inexorable Hispanization.[14] He believes, somewhat hazardously, that diverse peoples can give their loyalty to a single prince, provided that each people is, beneath the king's rule, represented justly by its optimates, either aristocratic or elected in assemblies.

Mariana is a distinctly bellicose theorist, or so it appears from his next chapter. He counsels a powerful army and the most modern fortifications as the preeminent bastions of the state. It is, of course, inconvenient that such an establishment is very costly and that funds to maintain it are difficult to extract from the assemblies of citizens. The Ship Money crisis, which contributed to the destruction of the English monarchy, lay in the future, but Mariana was aware of the form just such a crisis might take. His solution is not to weaken the armed forces, and so to subject Spain to the dangerous incursion of demobilized soldiers, but to engage them in virtually perpetual warfare and to allow "war to nourish war" by maintaining them on enemy soil. Ancient territorial claims can usually be found and renovated if present political situations justify no immediate attack. The monarch himself ought not to command his forces from a desk far behind the lines, but seek to maintain the reputation of a warrior in person. With the king and the aristocracy thus almost permanently on campaign, one can only suppose that Mariana envisages a state entirely in the hands of bishops on the home front.

If the chapter on war speaks of a situation that is eminently costly, the following one, on taxation, speaks of the most straitened economy. Mariana recognizes the state of affairs which actually exists: the people have little more to give in taxes, and the yield to be expected from the nobility is little more promising, even if it were possible to revoke their exemptions. Tax-farming is extortionate and counterproductive, so that really Mariana can propose little else than a new dependence on indirect taxation, particularly at ports of entry, and economies in royal disbursements of various kinds. The theme, which he is later to develop into a complete treatise, on the debasement of the coinage, finds its place here as well.

He inserts here two entirely conventional chapters on the selection of judges and the administration of the laws. Abstract considerations of virtue are invoked, but above all it is clear that Mariana has little interest in the subject apart from a general loathing for men of law, lay or ecclesiastical.

Far more enthusiasm goes into his consideration of how far the monarch ought to interest himself in the welfare of the poor. Mariana is extremely liberal, one might almost say modern, in his insistence that the great fortunes of Spain must be inexorably stripped down for the benefit of the poor and powerless. The clergy are by far the best equipped to secure this distribution through their ancient charity foundations, while the cities could cooperate best in suppressing vagabondage, a state of affairs that depletes the monies available for true relief.[15] The state should concentrate on measures for the future prevention of poverty at its source, by planned removal of indigent populations toward areas of Spain that are unproductive through lack of water policies. (This latter solution was, of course, only adopted with any diligence in the reign of Charles III, when new towns began to appear in south central Spain.) One discerns behind the proposals of Mariana the usual leitmotif of horror at the thought of rootless, disorderly populations with nothing to lose,[16] just as in his advocation of warfare to postpone the day when demobilized armies might make their way back to Spain.

The final chapter resumes what the prince ought to know of that preeminent Renaissance virtue, prudence. Naturally this contains the Christian cardinal virtue in all of its aspects. Mariana shows, however, that he has a lack of confidence in this alone as a guide to the conduct of the monarch's life in everyday politics and in the life of courts. He may have to concede a little to the otherwise anathematized precepts of Machiavelli: when to dissemble, when to temporize, when to measure out rewards and sanctions among his despicable entourage of courtiers. In this concession we may descry the devious lineaments of the superior man as he will be projected by a later Jesuit, Baltasar Gracián, forty years in the future.

The work has a kind of coda: an independent essay not especially directed to the prince, nor prescriptive of what a prince should necessarily do. It is rather Mariana's personal *parecer* on the matter of pluralism of religion within a single nation-state, nourished no doubt by his experience of the horrifying wars of religion in France. He observes that the strife inevitable in a religiously divided state will impel the prince toward tyranny, as it erodes the ancient traditions and institutions of either kingdom or republic, and as the deliberations of popular assemblies are held up interminably by the partisans of different sects. Even the family breaks down as wives and daughters adopt distinctive faiths and leave home to join their fellow sectaries. The beautiful and seductive word "liberty" has so often turned out to be specious and false; to allow total liberty of conscience and choice of religion is to be uncaring for the happiness of society.[17]

What *On the King* Deduces from History

Works of political theory throughout the Middle Ages had tended to present themselves as treatises closely dependent on theology. At least the style of discourse that gives them shape is that of the theologian. A slow development associated with the European Renaissance is the replacement of this style by others. The specialized vocabulary and attitude toward language of the jurisconsult, perhaps, or of the historian, were to become more usual. [18] In Mariana's case we may anticipate two things: his detestation and incomprehension of *leguleyos* (practicians of legal chicanery) will account for the small place that juridical considerations and vocabulary will have in his work; and identical attitudes and instances will be exploited in both *On the King* and *The General History of Spain*.

This allows Mariana to select among biblical, Roman, and modern monarchs for his examples of how the recipient of his *Institutio* ought and ought not to behave. As bad kings, who eventually or even immediately became tyrants, he prudently cites Nimrod, Tarquin, and Nero. It has been thought that these are evasively chosen names covering the real personality of Philip II. [19] Certainly in a famous passage he attributes the destruction of the Invincible Armada to the concupiscence of "a certain prince" (edition of 1605). Among good kings and their actions he singles out Henry III of Castile, who first overhears his courtiers as they boast of depleting the treasury, and then frightens them into submission; and Alfonso VIII and his exemplary punishment of the treacherous governor of Zorita. The same recourse to actual historical instances allows Mariana to counsel the rehabilitation of the powerful popular assemblies of earlier centuries, even though a strong imperial monarchy might seem *theoretically* more attractive; also the hereditary kingship, for all its irrationality, since elective promotion of political chiefs (Praetorian Guard; Comuneros) has *in the event* produced the more dire examples.

Monarch and Subjects in *On the King*

Mariana begins his study of the juridical stature of the kingly office with a supposition: that the first kings were men chosen by the weak and unprotected many. The power of kings may then be said to have emanated from the people, and this transmission of power has not been a warrant for considering it alienated from them:

Neque verisimile sit sua si cives universos penitus auctoritate spoliare voluisse, transferre in alium sine exceptione, sine consilio rationeque, quod necesse non erat, effecisse ut princeps corruptioni obnoxius et pravitati maiorem universis haberet potestatem; foetus parente, rivus origine praestantior?

(Nor would it be likely if he were to desire to divest the entire citizenry of its power for ever, and alienate it without consideration and without good reason. For would it be obligatory for them to accept that a prince capable of corrupt actions and of vicious living should have greater powers than all of them? Has the offspring preeminence over the parent, or the spring over the river it gives rise to?) (Chapter 8)

The monarch, then, does not stand above the laws, and the ruler who refuses to bridle himself as he does others becomes by that very course of action a tyrant. This was not a self-evident proposition in Mariana's age; an opposing idea had been current ever since the study of the possible applicability of Roman Law had begun in the Middle Ages. According to the chief Roman Law text, the *Institutes* of the Emperor Justinian, all legislative powers were to be considered handed over by the subjects to their emperor; he could choose to be truly *legibus solutus*.[20] This concept had been seen as a valuable weapon by both sides in the medieval Investiture Contest, between the papacy and the Holy Roman Empire, and its advantages had not been lost on subsequent monarchical regimes.

Mariana, of course, rejects this notion, preferring to regard the king as primary servant of the commonwealth; he derives this ultimately from St. Thomas Aquinas.[21] He proceeds to the question of whether, in less troubled times when the principle of authority has itself been removed from debate, the king ought perhaps to relinquish power to an oligarchy in a republican mode of government. He is scrupulously fair in his examination of this possible political process but he eventually shows he has a prevailing belief in the fallen nature of man; this obliges the commonwealth of men to accept kingly guardians. If such a guardian, of course, begins to demonstrate *his* fallen nature in injustice, then he must be unceremoniously replaced. Power derives, therefore, for Mariana, not from any quasi-priestly mystery conveyed to the king by his anointing or otherwise, nor from the community at large as the instrument of a theocracy (this is approximately the position of Suárez in his

De legibus ac Deo legislatore, 1612), but from the practicality of rule
by the best fitted, the king and the optimates, and this rule is
grounded in the principle of human sociability itself.[22]

The king must maintain himself in power, but differences in
human desires will stimulate rebellions against that power, or at
least political resistance. Mariana shows no special originality on
this point; few theorists of the time, Catholic or Protestant, ever
did. The preeminent rights of the Cortes help to canalize this resistance in a just state and render it benign. The king, like Fernando
the Catholic in the *General History,* will lose little by quietly "losing
face."[23] When the Cortes is incapable of rationalizing its resistance,
then the episcopal "ephors" will perform the function. Above all,
the king will strive to prevent all this by an efficient intelligence
service; he must know the truth: *Et sunt veritatis radices amarae,
fructus suavissimi* ("The roots of the truth are bitter, but their yield
of fruit is most sweet").[24] And no doubt among these "bitter roots"
were the torture-chambers and the unscrupulous secret agents of
that age. Mariana goes on to advise that when rebellion does occur,
in spite of all precautions, the king ought never to meet the insur-
gents face to face, and that once they are defeated he should make
no ostentatious examples of their ringleaders, but rather operate
enigmatically:

> Sedato tumultu quorum praecipua noxa erit, iis irrogare supplicia nihil
> vetabit, sed carptim ac singulis, quod ad consensum multitudinis exten-
> uendam saluberrimam remedium est.

> (Once the revolt is subdued nothing will prevent the king from imposing
> penalities on those who were chiefly responsible, but it must be myste-
> riously and only one at a time. This is a way of dealing with the task of
> innocuously lulling the opinion of the multitude.) (III, xiv)

Powers of deposing an unfit ruler and of arranging for his replacement by legitimate—or legitimized—succession is vested by
Mariana in the assembly of the governed. Hereditary succession, or
even de facto military hegemony, is not unreasonable, provided that
competent electors have sanctioned it. This will, however, always
be vitiated by the weakness inherent in any voting process: *Neque*

enim suffragia ponderantur, sed numerantur, ac ne fieri quidem aliter potest ("For votes are not weighed in the balance but rather merely counted, and nobody can ever change this circumstance" [I, ii]). It is remarkable in the political program of a Jesuit that he should not at any point suggest the possible intervention of the Pope to impose interdict and deposition of an incompetent monarch. On the contrary, he makes mention of the conciliar authority that invests, and in effect limits, the pontifical power itself.

Mariana's conception of the tyrant owes much, as we have earlier suggested, to the writings of St. Isidore, for example: . . . *ut cum quaeritur quid intersit inter regem et tyrannum, adiecta differentia, quid uterque sit definitur: id est, rex est modestus et temperans, tyrannus vero impius et immitis (Etymologies,* II:29:7: "If it be asked what separates a king from a tyrant, let it be defined in this way: a king is decent and temperate, while a tyrant is truly impious and ruthless"); *Iam postea in usum accidit tyrannos vocari pessimos atque improbos reges, luxuriosae dominationis cupiditatem et crudelissimam dominationem in populis exercentis (Etymologies,* IX:iii:20: "It is now also usual to call the worst and the wicked kings tyrants, those who inflict on the peoples their greed for lustful power and their most cruel autocracy").[25] Isidore in his turn probably derived his image of the tyrant from that which was a commonplace among the Roman historians: savagery, covetousness (especially with regard to temple-spoliation and incitement of troops to rapine), and sexual license.[26] The pessimistic addition to this outline of tyranny that Mariana makes is merely that the removal of a tyrant frequently makes a pathway for a similar ruler: Otho and Vitellius replace Nero. Also, to preempt powers and to debase currency are acts of tyranny different in degree but not in kind from violent spoliation by troops, in his view.

The violent removal of such a tyrant resembles, according to Mariana, something as noble as the defense of a wife or a mother against a violator. It does not matter whether the tyrant has seized power illegally or has degenerated while legally in office; the assembly of the governed has the immediate responsibility of impeaching him. If, however, the Cortes cannot assemble, either a conspiring committee or an individual patriot must act. Every care ought to be taken that this tyrannicide is not to be accomplished by a mere malcontent fanatic, and like Bellarmine and Suárez within his Society, Mariana exempts the clergy from the task.[27] There was for Mariana an awkward obstacle in the edicts of the Council of Constance in 1415, which imply that "not every tyrant may be killed before sentence has been pronounced on him," which would allow his rule to continue unchecked in many circumstances. Our author is inclined to circumvent the deliberations of that particular council, considering it very doubtfully an ecumenical one. He is, nevertheless, no Jacobin; no private citizen can be allowed the unqualified right to resist and depose. The trouble for many contemporaries of Mariana lay in the Jesuit insistence that an anathematized heretic ruler was ipso facto a sentenced tyrant.[28] Royalists quickly inferred that the Society was constituting itself the arbiter of which ruler was anathematized, and therefore vulnerable to murderous attack, and which not. Did not Mariana's book bear the Jesuit imprimatur? Should not all kings fear at least dethronement whether their "tyranny" compares with Henry III's or not?[29]

The question of poisoning the tyrant is really a trivial one, but Mariana certainly spends much time discussing it; it must, then, have not been a trivial one for him. The distinction between the swallowed and the smeared poison seems to us, as it did to Bayle, ridiculous and puerile. Our author is concerned that the act of being poisoned should not appear to be involuntary suicide; the victim has to raise the glass and could refuse it. Contact with a poisoned surface does not offer this inconvenience. The matter will no doubt never be clear, though some compunction connected with the path of the received species of the Eucharist through the mouth may lie behind it. Mariana is on the whole confident that his work will be more than anything a deterrent, rendering tyrannicide less frequent, and "palace revolutions" more attractive to discontented subjects of princes.

After all this attention given by Mariana to his topic a question surely occurs to the reader: Why the specific preoccupation with tyrants and their removal? Were there so many tyrants, in political terms, at that moment in European history? From the point of view of many observers the most tyrannous in their time had been the father of the prince to whom *On the King* is dedicated, the recently dead Philip II himself. No other name would come to mind. The discussion, then, appears to emanate from theoretical "monarchomach" speculations alone; it was what *could* happen if kings were to become more absolute.[30] In the event, after Mariana's work had begun to have influence, it was the nontyrants who acquired a knowledge of how not to attempt the consolidation of their power. They behaved better, but they also became secularized rulers in secularized states. And constitutions, in times not too far ahead, began to assist in making tyranny unworkable.

The Supports of the State

As Mariana visualizes him, the monarch has duties: to protect innocence, to provide safety, to punish wickedness, and to extend the power of his kingdom to increase beneficence and felicity. But for this to succeed he requires a toiling multitude of assistants, cooperating with him in his divine mandate; "both prince and council are God's vicegerents here on earth," as Fadrique Furió Ceriol had put it.[31]

The task of recruiting new elites becomes therefore of special importance for the king. On the one hand the education of the most promising of the youth must be promoted by their parents, and inspected by lay commissioners on the king's behalf, and on the other hand the best in their adulthood ought to be compelled, if necessary, to serve their community. Among these the common people are more fitted to serve the king than an ancient nobility; through concern for livelihoods they may be controlled:

Syncerius solent populares iudicare; potentiores ad gratiam saepe loquuntur, studiaque fere utilitate magis quam veritate metiri solent; eos commendantes maxime unde maior emolumenti spes affulserit.

(Men of the people usually make more honest judgments; the more powerful often speak favorably, yet usually perform their tasks more out of a concern for expediency than for personal integrity. Those in whom the hope of greater reward shines more brightly are especially to be recommended.) (III, iii)

These rewards (and, when necessary, punishments) produce the best servants of the state, and at the same time promote social cohesion. Careers are, and are seen to be, open to talent. What Mariana apparently does not foresee is the probability of a multiplication of offices, but since the king is envisaged as presenting the list of appointable men for popular selection, he no doubt assumes that this is in itself a control.[32] Other means of selection current in our author's day he insists must be discontinued, notably the criterion of *limpieza de sangre* (a test imposed to exclude all but Old Christians), which is divisive and pernicious.

When he speaks of "the people" Mariana does not, of course, mean *el vulgo* ("the proletariat"), and in fact says so. He is very aware, however, that the body of small cultivators and tenant farmers of Castile largely supports the whole edifice of the state. Their procurators, though they may be men of limited talents and vision, should always be consulted by the monarch and his counselors. At least the monarch should carefully appear to be consulting them; his reverence for the laws ought to be as visible in this matter as in that of obeying sumptuary edicts he has himself proclaimed. It will be observed how reluctant Mariana is, nevertheless, to have this consultative process consolidated into a constitution; this would give leverage within the state to the detested men of law *(leguleii),* those who "have so mired the stable that Hercules could not now cleanse it."

The king must, at bottom, accustom all his subjects to the principle of sharing. Even robbers do this, so why not honest men? This should help to resolve the spirit of faction, which has its basis in diversity of national origin and social class. Mariana follows, as we have seen, the prescriptions of Furió Ceriol in recommending a random choice of candidates from all provinces of the monarchy for offices high and low. Hannibal, as he puts it, called all valiant captains Carthaginians. The powerful must be forced to hold unsalaried office, and to support companies of troops, while the powerless must eventually disappear: for civil peace nobody should have nothing to lose. The subsuming terror of the age can be discerned, that of the multiplying rootless poor swamping the cities, there to be joined by the demobilized troops returning with their nihilistic

Landsknecht mentality from the incessant wars.[33] Compelling all to share becomes not just a fine Christian precept but a policy of sheer prudence.

For his own times Mariana is pessimistic, with reservations:

> Oculos in universam provinciam extendite, plures integros magistratus, sacerdotes sanctos, proceres modestos inveniatis. Sed in eo quoque natura prava est: facilius pravitas paucorum occurrit memoriae, quam multorum innocentia. Quod si mentem a proximis annis, quibus sua quoque inerant vitia, ad paulo superiora referatis, bella intestina, procerum dissidia, promiscuam libidinum licentiam, stupra, caedes, peculatus, rapinas, in regia ipsa suppositos partus, regentium ignaviam, fortassis multo commodiora nostra tempora fateamini, longo intervallo discrepare ab illis.

> (Cast your eyes over every land and you will find many upright ministers, devout clergymen, virtuous nobles. But there also nature is vile; the villainy of the few strikes the memory more easily than the innocence of the many. For if you cast your mind back from the most recent times, which have also known their vices, to those a little removed, you will observe civil strife, treason among the nobles, free rein given everywhere to lust, rapes, murders, frauds, robberies, concealed births in the very regal palace, sloth among the ruling party, perhaps you will pronounce our age to be much healthier and much different from those former times.) (Preface to *De morte,* 360)

The supports of the state, we observe, alone guarantee its keeping clear of degeneration under a new regime.

Religious, Military, and Fiscal Bonds of the State

The absence in Mariana's theory of the state of strong juridical bonds as the basis of legislative rights causes him to appear to look elsewhere for the groundwork of the social nexus. As a member of the clergy he could be expected to advance the cause of the Church and of organized religion as a trustworthy factor. It is a matter of "hygiene" for him that there should be unity of religion in the kingdom;[34] in this his anxieties coincide with those of the Holy Office of the Inquisition, but he cannot bring himself to condone the latter's methods. It is no doubt a matter of the same detestation of delation that we have seen him expressing in his complaint against the Society. The obstinacy of Jews and heterodox Christians (he makes no mention of Muslim minorities, even in the decade of the expulsion of the Moriscos) is an affront to him, but coercion by the monarch would be an even greater one. He does not advocate toleration, though he had to endure censure of his promotion of "liberty, that virtue which usually is affected by villainy" in years to come.[35] He does, however, deal with a concrete case in the *History:* The obscure and possibly heterodox writings of Ramon Llull might, in their day, have been profitably overlooked by Pope Gregory XI.[36] Pontifical concern led to their being taken up by enthusiasts, whereas neglect would have consigned them to dust along with other dull books. It would have been hard, however, for the Inquisition to have "neglected" to prosecute Judaizers and Protestants in the seventeenth century. The problem of what Mariana would have proposed remains a problem.

In the final chapter of *On the King* Mariana comes close to implying that the state religion need not necessarily be Catholicism. The king may not select a religion at will, however, so we must presume that the existing majority religion will be insisted upon. From that point there must be no dissenters, or civil peace will become incapable of maintenance. Nobles will, as happened in France in Mariana's view, dissent as a pretext for rebellion; plebeian malcontents will not be restrained from attacking their oppressors (and then moving to make short work of the Church); finally there will be foreign intervention. Toleration just is not worth it. He is aware of foreign states where it exists: many cantons of Switzerland (but the Swiss are opportunistic mercenaries anyway) and the Ottoman Empire (but there atrocities occur on *every other* score; a Jew or a Greek Christian may be free to worship, but is in bondage nevertheless to a heinous tyrant).

The strong position of the Church, under its able leaders the bishops chosen by the king, as the nucleus of the state will entail its increased financial autonomy and stewardship. Mariana is quite aware of the centuries of criticism the Church had endured on account of its riches and lands. He prefers to think about these riches positively, as having been the key to much internal colonization and much aid given to the state in its previous wars. He is indignant at the way kings have despoiled the Church of wealth—wisely choosing remote medieval instances rather than the massive encroachments of Philip II. The Church's stewardship is not, as so many believe, a "dead hand," but rather a stimulus to able clerics to show virtue. He does concede that state auditors should "make a show" of going through the Church's account books. He does not make much of a point of monies going to Rome; Peter II of Aragon refused to pay tribute to the Holy See, and Mariana seems to approve of his refusal. The "curialist" argument of the *potestas directa* of the Pope finds no advocate in him.[37]

Finally, with regard to religion, the king himself would do well to be pious, but not of course superstitious. It can free him from many anxieties of his office and strengthen his equanimity.

Mariana can evidently see in the future king's reign nothing but a state and a church equally embattled, the affairs of Europe being what they are. He hopes therefore for a harmony of outlook between churchmen and high officials, both civil and military. So that militarism becomes one of the bonds of the state: *Prima ergo cura principis sit ut bellum seipsum alat* ("The first concern of the prince shall be that war nourish war"). The distinction between just wars and merely profitable ones is scarcely drawn by this bellicose Jesuit; the myth of past crusades and former chivalry is allowed to blur the issue. Martial Spain must be revived, and financed if necessary by plunder, especially that of the "cities of the impious," while all coastal communities should be prepared to engage in privateering. One observes a complete adherence to the ideas of Machiavelli, and a correspondingly complete alienation from Erasmus, in this desperate bid to provide a unitary texture for the state.[38]

What profitable wars cannot provide as an economic basis for the state, taxation must. But the king who imposes taxes on his own initiative is a potential tyrant from that very moment. Deficit financing and its equivalent, debasement of the buying power of currency in circulation, are anathema to Mariana, so the taxation of productive land is to be uniquely recommended. In fairly paternalistic fashion large landholders are to be regulated by continuous state inspection; smaller cultivators are to compete for valuable subsidies. Public works will be financed from the productivity of the relevant districts. Tax exemptions that are relics of the Reconquista should slowly disappear. Except that Mariana has no conception of the thorny problem of assessing fair agricultural prices, the whole plan seems quite modern,[39] if perhaps a little sentimental.[40]

Mariana the moralist is at odds with Mariana the economist over the question of luxury trades. These are an undeniable source of wealth, both within Spain and without (for Mariana has grasped the notion of balance of payments), yet they carry the danger of social dissolution; the lower classes soon wish to enjoy the advantages of coaches and silken apparel when they eventually have money. "Private vices, public benefits" is a horrid maxim from Mariana's point of view, but human nature being what it is, *quod si sanari noluerint, ex eorum fructu aliquem ad rempublicam redire aequum erit* ("if they cannot be cured of it will be reasonable that something should accrue to the state from those profits," III, vii). This is rather like what he wearily concedes in the matter of brothels and bullfights in his other treatise. Labor-intensive projects like the Escorial have their uses and in their way symbolize the cohesion, religious, military, and economic, which underlies the state.[41]

We may theorize, then, that this threefold endeavor at cohesion is imagined by Mariana because he gives so low a value to juridical cohesion. The absence of the legal framework—except for purely practical matters in the courts—places Mariana already close to the theorists of reason of state *(razón de estado)* and of the beneficent absolutist ruler.[42]

On the King and the Ravaillac Affair

It is notorious that when the archives in the Royal Palace of the kings of France on the Île de la Cité in Paris were consumed in flames in 1618 the truth about the murder of Henry IV by François Ravaillac eight years earlier was made forever inaccessible. There were even those who claimed that unidentifiable accomplices of the assassin started the fire. All we can do is situate the murder in a period of French, and Jesuit, politics. We can also for practical purposes exonerate the confused enthusiast Ravaillac *(ce malheureux,* as the Jesuit Father Coton called him),[43] and also note that Mariana himself had nothing to say about the assassination.

Two independent phenomena were determining the conduct of affairs in the immediate entourage of the French kings. First there was an accumulation of abstract speculation on the limits of monarchy, which is usually attributed to the "monarchomachs,"[44] some of whom were Huguenots and Politiques, and who were ultimately combating in their writings the same potential for tyranny that the Jesuits like Rivadeneira were warning of. Inevitably they acquired opponents, who tended to exalt the monarchy by insisting on a doctrine, with copious biblical authority, of Divine Right. The other phenomenon was the polarization of warring parties for and against the king, Henry III. After undeniably tyrannous acts such as the murder of his opponent the Duke of Guise, Henry III was excommunicated and himself murdered by Jacques Clément. Mariana notoriously *seems to have* approved the murder ten years after the event: *Clemens, . . . aeternum Galliae decus ut plerisque visum est* ("Clément, an eternal ornament of France, in the majority's view" [the phrase was expunged from the 1611 edition]). But he does not actually align himself with the alleged "majority view." There was a kind of coalescence, in the event; opponents of the monarchomachs found themselves defending the memory of Henry III, and fearing for the safety of the new king, Henry IV, though he was now no longer a heretic and therefore unlikely to be called a tyrant by Jesuit political writers.

Ravaillac's was not the first attempt to assassinate Henry IV. Already in 1593 there had been the Barrière affair, when the Jesuits were implicated in at least the suspicion of having helped in a plot. In the event it led to Barrière's execution and a clamor for the expulsion of the Society from France as Philip II's agents.[45] The next year came the Chastel affair, which led to searches of the Society's archives. Father Guignard was found to have written a memorandum containing praise for Jacques Clément and more clamor ensued. Chastel also suffered execution and Father Guéret, S.J., who had conversed with him on the subject of tyrannicide, was exiled. The whole Society became alarmed and proclaimed from Rome its collective innocence and esteem for France's king. When

in 1599 *On the King* appeared, the Jesuit general, Acquaviva, already
was diffident about the passage on Clément, but did nothing ac-
tively, and the book had little real currency outside the libraries of
the Society, where its discussion of tyrannicide would certainly have
no novelty. The Society received permission in 1603 to return to
France and to the court itself.

Ravaillac, it appears, acted entirely alone in the religious sphere.
His contacts had always been more frequent with other orders,
seldom with any Jesuit. His knowledge of Latin, his general literacy,
and his mental equilibrium were all inadequate for a true understanding of the book he was alleged to have read. His stated reasons
for doing away with Henry IV were probably accurate: the Pope had
condemned the execution of Chastel, and Parlement had had the
brief publicly burned, so Ravaillac blamed Henry IV in his ignorance
of the relation of powers within the state. In his view, Henry should
have forcibly converted all Huguenots at the moment of his own
conversion. Also the king, he had heard, was intending to march
on Rome and forcibly remove the Holy See to Paris. Finally, for
Ravaillac the papacy and God were identical, and he understood
that the people were with him. The question of whether Henry was
steered by others toward Ravaillac is insoluble, and the fire of 1618
leaves everything in the area of speculation.[46]

Immediately after the murder *On the King* received the blame; it
was alleged to have contained advocacy of regicide. The Sorbonne
began to promulgate the doctrines of Divine Right and of nonre-
sistance,[47] and succeeded in having the work of Mariana ceremonially
burned on June 8 of the same year in front of the cathedral of Notre
Dame itself, after having been transported there alone in a special
cart attended by court ushers. Pope Paul V and General Acquaviva
both disowned the book and anathematized regicide in any circumstances, except those of the Acts of the Council of Constance: the
heroic killing of a proven tyrant.[48] Unfortunately, at the same time
the Jesuit Robert Bellarmine published his political treatise advocating pontifical deposition and outlawry of heretical monarchs
(something Mariana had never gone so far as to advocate). It too fell
victim to the royalist rage of the Parlement of Paris.[49]

The Ravaillac affair coincided with the saddest time in Mariana's life: his trial and imprisonment in Madrid. His fellow Jesuits nobly defended his book at the time, but their support slowly eluded him afterwards, no doubt because news of his *parecer* on the ills of the Society was becoming known.[50] Truly it had been "one of the days that made France," but it ensured the confusion of tyrannicide and regicide—a confusion indispensable to absolute monarchs—and the neglect of the other proposals contained in the book.

What *On the King* Is Not

Mariana is emphatically no democrat; the common man seems to make him depressed: *Quid miserius quam in populi insania partem aliquam felicitas constituere?* ("What is more miserable than for one's happiness to have any part in the velleity of the people?").[51] He allows great authority to the *universa respublica,* it is true, but the extending of this to the great commonalty is more the proposal of Suárez (*De legibus,* 1612; *Defensio fidei,* 1613). His great subject is more truly authority, springing as it does from ancient roots in Castile,[52] eroded in its institutions but not to be replaced by any other of constitutional type. This nationalism of outlook is indeed present; Castile, with its weak middle and artisan classes since *co-munero* times, is the model Mariana works to.

And of course Mariana cannot be loved by any royalist. He has "hollowed out" the kingly office and the king's very person more than any other theorist who is not simply a republican. Kings are for him secular and utilitarian beings, incapable of capturing the irrational regard of the masses. Myths, rituals and symbolism have no place in the secular world for any of these Jesuit preceptors, whereas the great royalist theorists (Bolingbroke, *The Idea of a Patriot King* [1749]; Jacques Mallet du Pan, *Considérations sur la nature de la Révolution en France* [1793]; Novalis, *Glauben und Liebe* [c. 1797]; even the more practical Walter Bagehot, *On the Monarchy* [1865])[53] make these irrational considerations—and the virtue that monarchy has of disguising real power held by others—the nucleus of their pleas for the conservation of the immemorial institution.

Chapter Four

On Immortality and Other Topics

A Colloquy of Consolation

Perhaps it was in the spring of 1601 that a friend of Mariana's, whom we know only by the Latinized name of Castellionius (possibly Castellón or Castejón), and who was apparently a judicial officer of the Inquisition and a desultory poet and a man of letters, suffered a saddening bereavement. His wife died while giving birth to a daughter, who also died almost immediately. The reflections on mortality this event stirred in Mariana provide the substance of his "De morte et immortalitate" [On Death and Immortality], the most varied in content, as it happens, of the *Seven Treatises*.

The long conversation that lends its form to the work—really a set of talks by Mariana himself, sometimes formal lectures, sometimes causeries of more aimless type interrupted by his hearers—probably actually took place at the two named locations, one of the Cigarrales (suburban estates) near Toledo and the village of Carmena farther out in the country, at the beginning of May. Those taking part in Toledo were Castellón, Mariana, and a Dean (Decanus); in Carmena we read of the intervention of the priest of the place, Juan Ferrera, and his brother Francisco. The Classical model for the work is, of course, the Ciceronian dialogue, such as *On Friendship* or *On Old Age*—the dialogue of consolation which Cicero wrote after the death of his own daughter Tullia has not come down to us.[1]

A distinction has been made between the dialogues of antiquity and those of the Renaissance. In the earlier ones that have survived, the authors' initial opinions seem to predominate, and the interlocutors are permitted to explore these; they are presented above all as intelligences, not as rounded personalities. In the dialogues of the Renaissance at their best it is not unusual to read of the speakers expressing doubts, irrelevances, or hesitations—that is, simulating the art of conversation as it occurs in life, or in fiction. A speaker's idiosyncrasies can be discerned, and this helps us to sketch a portrait, however exiguous, in our mind's eye, to associate with the voice intervening in the work.[2] Castellón, in spite of his mourning, provides an erudite joke; we may infer that in happier days he was a man of good humor.[3] The Dean is rather the good clubman, fond of the wholesome conversation—into which he obtrudes no exceptionable opinions of his own—of the country setting, and above all of the meals (*"Tum Decanus, . . . dum paratur prandium . . ."* [p. 386] is a very usual conjunction of terms). Ferrera represents another type of the good-natured man; he finds it unfeeling on the part of Providence that man should bear such punishment for Original Sin, and has to permit correction by the more strictly doctrinaire Mariana.[4] There seems to be some reticent humor in Mariana's presentation of himself, as the patient "anchor-man" keeping his interlocutors' minds on the subject, and as conscious of his reputation for inurbanity; at least one supposes he means it in jest when he includes in a colloquy of consolation for a distraught widower the remark that a marriage has only two happy days, the first and the last!

Just as we have seen him do in the case of *On the King,* Mariana provides here a lavish series of settings amid bountiful nature. In this he is conforming to the rhetorician's requirement of "topothesia,"[5] somewhat related to the "composition of place" of the Ignatian *Exercises,* and likewise intended to affect the state of mind of the reader. If this is almost a paradise on earth, how much more splendid must be what awaits the attainer to immortality! These long passages of prose-poetry occur in the exordium and at moments of linkage between conversations. Mariana describes a natural landscape in heightened terms, with all imperfections omitted and with its constituent features arranged into an aesthetically attractive order. There is an insistence on purling streams both among the Cigarrales and at Carmena, and on the ways in which countrymen enhance the scenery by their diligence. Yet it is a recognizably Castilian landscape, not the accumulation of symbolic images that turns up so often in works of art and literature in Mariana's time.[6]

Our author gives us in effect a geographer's or an agronomist's view of the region over which the *suburbana praedia* (country homes outside the city), those called Los Cigarrales, are built. He observes as he goes the scarcity of water and the poor management of what little water there is. Orchards are numerous, but their cultivators scarcely "break even" *(Proventus exiguus ac vix culturae impensam exaequans)* because of this. Mariana describes his visit to the simple but artistically decorated villa, where trees are planted correctly in quincunxes amid formal gardens. The manager *(herus)* has allowed a conduit to be made and the gardens are expected to become fruitful as a result. Here Mariana the chemist remarks on the presence of pseudojacinth in the rocks, a mineral which always cleanses the water that percolates through it. The completed works are considered worthy of celebration by the adaptation of a Greek epigram into Latin:

> Tres hospes charites his hortis cernis inesse:
> Urbis prospectus prima venustas erat;
> Arboribus, villae, haustris iuncta est altera et herbis;
> Quid reliquam? Ferro saxa cavata tenent.

(You will observe three excellences in these gardens: the first fine feature is the view of the city; the second comprises the trees, the villa, the vases and the greensward; what do I omit? The conduits chiseled into the rocks.)

Over the years the Society of Jesus has acquired an estate with two villas close to each other. At the upper one, close by the military road, is the farm. This allows Mariana to describe its animals and implements, rendering it all as in a seventeenth-century genre picture in prose. Here are the sleeping quarters, the dining loggia *(porticus epulis destinata)*, and the small chapel.

The lower house lies in a wood; it is quieter and better adapted for study and lectures. Mariana describes passing the night there and his elation at being awakened by birds of many species:

Aviculae consono cantu quasi de victoria certare lucis adventatis honore laetae: cardueles, chlores, philomelae, ante omnes cuculus e villae fastigio raucum cantum edens et funebre contendere de peritia cum caeteris aviculis videbatur, provocare ad certamen homine iudice superbus sibique nimium confidens. Sic est nemo orator, poeta, centor se alium meliorem putat, neque de peritia cuiquam concedit. Hoc etiam malis contingit.

(The little birds [could be heard] in harmonious song, as though they were happy to strive for the honor of celebrating the victory of approaching light: goldfinches, greenfinches, linnets, and above all others the cuckoo, singing forth his hoarse note from the rooftop of the villa, competing in skill against the other birds, and proud to provoke them in his overweening self-confidence, with man as the arbiter. It is exactly in this way that nobody—orator, poet, or singer—ever accepts that someone may possess greater skill than he does himself, and assumes he is superior to all others. This can be very unattractive.) (385)

The scents of morning flowers give joy to his sense of smell, and soon he has picked a basketful from the pleasance, a true *locus amoenus* with all its plants lovingly listed by name.[7] He meets the Dean and Castellionius as they arrive in their conveyance *(carpento vehi . . . vidimus)*, and they proceed to an early celebration of Mass. But the narrative soon returns to the nagging hydraulic question and to the unreliability of water engineers: *Aquileges deceperunt genus hominum fallax quod semper vituperabitur et semper vigebit* ("Water engineers were untrustworthy—an unreliable breed of humanity who will always draw down wrath and who will never change their ways"). There is a fishpond, however, and the three men sit by it observing the fishes and avoiding the sun beneath surrounding trees. They discuss the day's agenda, and Mariana is able to assure the Dean that the colloquies of the day will be divided by an ample lunch hour *(bifarium potius dividatur)*. They go indoors, stand before the three windows for a while *(ad tres caeli plagas totidem fenestrae* ["three windows opening out on to as many sections of the sky," 387]), then settle upon the brickwork *poyo* or fixed bench to hear Mariana's first talk.

The pages of linkage between the sessions of the colloquy *On Death and Immortality* also contain evidence of Mariana's interest in sports and games. There are organized games both outside Toledo and at Carmena. The details of these and of the rules for winning may be of interest to the historian of Spanish rural customs:[8]

Varii erant parati ludi, tesserae, latrunculi, pilae, globi lignei cum circulo
ferreo in terra compacto, quem transmittant ac imprimis mensae longae
impositae tabulae rotundae pars nigrae pars candidae; quibus iactis magno
saepe nisu, quae propius ad extremum mensae marginem accedebant, nisi
impelletur ab adversaria, pro ea victoria stabat. Ludunt adversus singulos
singuli, aut plures etiam utrimque numero pugnantium exaequato. In-
struuntur adversae acies; incalescit pugna. Uno saepe ictu et impetu multi
hostes cadunt, variant secundae adversaeque res. Alea prorsus aberat, quon-
iam is ludus religiosos et modestos parum decet, quippe profanus, et in
quo maior sorti locus sit, quam industriae, neque corpus exerceatur, quae
praecipua ludi virtus est.

(Several games had been organized, chess, board-games, ball-games, and
a game with wooden spheres with an iron ring set in the ground. This
they must cast the ball through along a long table with round panels,
black and white, fixed to it. When the throw is made, often after a great
stride, the balls which lie closest to the far edge of the table, unless they
are propelled back by the opposite side, are counted as the winners. This
game was played either with one to a side, or with equal numbers on each
side of the contenders. The opposing lines are drawn up, and the contest
becomes heated. Often many fall after one strike, the advantage goes to
the other, opposing side. Dice were notably absent, since that game is
hardly fitting for religious and decent men, being indeed abominable and
one in which luck has the larger place, and not skill. Neither does it
exercise the body, a chief virtue of sports.) (p. 359)

Here is the description of skittles as played at Carmena in 1601:

. . . iuvenes videmus cum clamore et plausubolis ludentes, paxillos
teretes prosternere magno ornatu certantes.

Ratio lusus is est: novem paxilli querni torno perfecti in summo solo
recti extant, terni quoque versus paribus inter ipsos intervallis. Gemini
item querni globi adhibentur capitis magnitudine. Ii ex aliquanto spatio
manu rotantur a ludentium quoque in paxillorum ordines singuli deinceps
nisu non magno, ne longius procurrant. Qui gemina iactu, eo, et quem
e loco repetunt, ubi globus substitit, plures paxillos prostravit, is se iuvenis
victorem fert, palmam dexteritatis et praemium victoriae.

(We see some youths playing amid great shouting and cheering at a
game of knocking down some smooth pegs.

The rules of this game are: nine well-turned oaken pegs are set upright on the ground, at even intervals three by three. A pair of oaken balls the size of a man's head are employed. These are bowled from the hand by one of the players at a time from a certain distance and after a short stride, lest they travel too far, against the rows of pegs. Whoever after both throws, since they repeat the throw from the same place, has knocked down most pegs at the point where the ball stops, is declared the winner. That youth carries off the palm of dexterity and the prize of victory.) (418)

The works of man, his incessant beautification of the landscape and his making it fruitful for posterity, alternatingly considered beside the artless sports of youthful villagers, are part of the consolation Mariana is offering to Castellionius. This is what survives, and, as we shall see later, something like this awaits the virtuous beyond the grave.

The layout of the text of the treatise is threefold: "On the contempt we ought to show for death," "On the immortality of the soul and on Divine Providence," and "On the devout life." The thirteen chapters of the second part are bisected exactly by a storm scene, followed immediately by a brightening of the heavens:

Ad fontem qui in medio scatet ire pergebamus, cum repente nubibus caelum obductum, caligine lux involvitur tetra ac minaci. Inter ortum et Aquilonem vehemens ventus cum fulgetris et caeli fragore violento ac repentino flatu aspirabat. . . . Post horae spatium sedata procella pulsis nubibus et caligine diem sol restituit. E metu recreati intra villam silentio assedimus laeti.

(We were walking towards the spring which gushes forth in the middle of the place when suddenly the sky became covered in clouds and the light was blotted out by an ugly and threatening gloom. A strong wind from the northeast sprang up, accompanied by lightning and quakings in the heavens. . . . After an hour the sun brought back its light, the storm was over and the clouds were put to flight. Recovered from our fright we gladly sat down inside the quiet villa.) (397–98)

It can be demonstrated that this storm scene has a significance for how we are to read the second section of *On Death and Immortality*: before it Mariana had been discoursing on rational attitudes that men might take up with regard to immortality as a philosophical problem; in the latter half of the middle section it becomes apparent that the action of the storm has been to dispel the rational and to introduce the teachings of divine revelation on the subject, declared by the Old Testament God who "rides on the wings of the storm."

Mariana's first contribution to the conversation, "On the Contempt in Which We Should Hold Death," is an ascetic discourse with no especially Christian tendency. This sets the whole work apart from the venerable *ars moriendi* ("art of making a good end") tradition, which Mariana's fellow Jesuit St. Robert Bellarmine, for instance, was to continue in 1620 with his *De arte bene moriendi.* In Mariana's work, we may observe, there is no mention of the subversive arts of the Devil or of Purgatory, and the discussion of Divine Grace is carried on in a curiously detached (and doubtfully orthodox) manner, when we consider the content of the rest of the treatise. He is really discussing those aspects of the topic of immortality which might well be encountered in the works of pagan philosophers: "Each Day We Die," "A Long Life Harmed Many a Man," and "The Common Miseries of Living" are examples of the stages through which Mariana's thread of consolation passes.

The exordium presents us with Mariana trying to reason, rather unfeelingly, with the sorrowing Castellionius: Is not the fear of death more proper to pregnant women? Listen to their everyday conversation; are they not usually discussing it? Life makes us all labor under tedium and nausea, so that death is to be welcomed as a relief. We tend to fear the unknown, and death frightens us just as do objects we half-glimpse in the dark:

> Idem in morte accidit terribilis est non vi sua sed propter circumfusas opinionum tenebras et spectra absona ab atra bile commota. Inter noctis tenebras omnia terribilia apparent: arbores, lapides, iumenta, ipsi amici et propinqui monstra quaedam immania videntur, lucem expecta, ne loco movearis hisce larvis ne cedas. Puerorum instar cognatos et familiares timemus, si larvatos eosdem persona deposita amplectimur.

> (That the same thing should be true of death is not because of its own attributes but because of gloomy opinions surrounding it and the dire phantoms worked up by our black bile. In the darkness of night everything

looks frightening: trees, rocks, domestic animals, even our friends and neighbors appear to be uncanny monsters. So we are anxious for the light; we dare not move from the spot lest these specters come toward us! Like children, we fear even known and familiar persons if they grapple with us while playing at being ghosts, with masks on.)

And we risk a hundred forms of death every day: earthquakes, lightning, even from eating melons and figs. In fact many more have died untimely deaths from these trivial causes than from the violence of nature. A certain contempt for death, on the other hand, has always been the mark of the great captains and the martyrs. The important thing is to have distinguished well ahead of time what are the truly imperishable things, which are the attributes of mortal life one ought to have thrown off and which to have retained at the end. Most of the things mortals prize and envy others for possessing are false goods and are usually exchangeable for wealth. Added to this, the deviation into pleasures assures disasters; fame and honors impose a constant servitude; the married state is quite attractive in theory, but in practice it is deceptive for too many who have entered it: *Acute quidam primum et postremum diem nuptiarum optandum dixit, caeteros repudiandos* ("He was an astute man who declared that the first and last days of marriage are to be sought, the rest to be rejected," 368). To have achieved high station is no consolation; Mariana cites the dead Philip II, his queens, and Don Carlos, *stirpis maximu*[s], *in spem paterni regni natu*[s] *educatu*[s]*que* ("of the highest lineage, born and trained in the hope of attaining to his father's throne," 370).

Yet one can truly prepare for death by dealing mortal wounds in advance to the passions, and by surrendering to death only a body already weakened by asceticism. Mariana compares this with the tactics of the inhabitants of besieged Numantia, who destroyed before their collective death everything the Roman enemy might parade in triumph. So the miseries of life are ultimately beneficial: *Proinde si sapimus, si res ferent, carceres, catenas, tormenta, dolores, morbos non modo sustenebimus, sed vetro etiam provocabimus, quo cumulatior sit fructus* ("Hence if we know, if these things hold, prisons, fetters, torture, pain and diseases are not just endured by us, but we indeed reach out to them as to a cover of glass by virtue of which the fruit grows more abundantly," 444).

The soul, however, survives death. Mariana's analogy is with the fetus, which can survive the mother's death, or with Jonah's emerging. Really it is more of a metamorphosis, and alchemical change: *occulta et altiori chalchymia arte* ("by some strange and mysterious chemical art," 339 [*sic* for 439]). The dead, Mariana then believes he has proved, have no need of mourning.

Mariana, who has hitherto in the treatise shown himself as an ascetic and a despairer of human transcendence, moves to the exploration of the Christian metaphysic, and becomes quite jubilant at the prospect he sees. This is an oscillation we may observe throughout the work, in which he is following the play of his own mind alone; in his other works his intelligence moved to someone else's command. We may regret we have so few pages that are in this way illuminated by the mind of the essayist, comparable here and there to that, *ondoyant et divers,* of his great contemporary Montaigne.

He assimilates the immortal soul to the *ingenium,* mind in all its subtlety. In his age he points out that the creative spirit is ever advancing: new discoveries are being made in the production of foods, in medicine, printing, metallurgy and the fine arts. He tries to explain some mathematics to the Dean, connecting it to the age-old Pythagorean notion of primal number:

—. . . Numeris ergo elementa ligantur. An hoc clarum est?
—Clarius, inquit Decanus, aut perpetuis in tenebris caligamus.
—Explico, inquam, quae mathematicis tamen explorata sunt. . . .

("The elements [Mariana means fire, water, air and earth] are bound together by numbers. Have I made this clear?"
"Make it clearer," said the Dean, "or we shall be stumbling in perpetual darkness."
"I shall explain," I said, "for these things have indeed been examined by mathematicians. . . ." (139)

But the Dean still has difficulty in following metaphysical mathematics. Again, he is naively scandalized when Mariana permits himself a poeticized view of the afterlife: the antique heroes after their lives of virtue attained seats in the heavens. The Dean supposes that Mariana thinks this is literally true, although he has already had it pointed out to him that pagan notions of the afterlife are comparable to infants' food, made easy to swallow. A little more discussion of the topic of what survives death is soon interrupted by the storm.

The talk after this, as we have seen, turns to the topic of Divine Providence. Mariana argues the existence of God from design; the divine principle is no other than Chrysippus's force of necessity within nature or than Zeno's divine law or *anima mundi*. Part of the divine plan is that we may make our exit from the corporeal life, exchanging a mud dwelling for a marble one, like the snake, which loses its old skin by extruding itself through a narrow and rough place. One of the most striking passages in the whole of *On Death* is Mariana's description of Paradise, the marble dwelling, covering some five closely printed pages. It is, of course, a traditional heaven, a reflection of earth without earth's uglinesses and vexations:

> Quid vero quod terrae magnam partem squalida siccitate loca, rupes horridae et saxa tenent, saltus et montes impediunt ibicibus ferisque aliis et alitibus modo pervii, paludes, aestuaria operiunt terras exiguo saepe fructu. In caelo nihil horridum, nihil incultum, aut incolis vacuum.

> (Whereas truly rough places occupy with their aridity a great part of the earth, abrupt outcrops of rock and steep places, glens and heaths, only passable to mountain goats and other animals and birds, lie in the way, and marshes and arms of the sea shut off tracts of land often of low fertility. In heaven, however, nothing is abrupt, nothing is untilled or devoid of inhabitants.) (419)

This would seem to be a curious prospect of the earth against which to evoke a landscape of the beyond. We might call it a vision of Spain without the works of man; tillage and occupation—we cannot know for what purpose—help to define paradise. The landscape of the supraterrestrial is thereupon described. It transcends the human, but more strikingly it transcends the plebeian:

> Si in terris quam servis, damnatis exilio hominibus, multisque animantibus Deus domicilio destinavit, multa sunt specie et pretio admiranda, quae oculos et animos ad se rapiant, gemmae quasi ludentis naturae pulchra

colorum varietate, metalla pretiosa, aurum et argentum quae cupiditas
insanos homines agit, arbores onustae pomis, nucibus, glandibus, herbae
odoratae, flores specie admiranda, aviculae cantu et plumis conspicuae,
ferae in sylvis lustrisque suis, pecora et armenta per montes errantia, gem-
mati amnes amoeno riparum vestitu, arte excitata palatia caeli aemula,
signa, statuae, vestes illusae et rigentes auro; quid credamus in caelo fac-
tum, unde quasi guttae terrestria omnia e copioso thesauro liquantur, ut
ubi Deus et maiestatis suae palatium, et beatorum omnium esse voluit.

(If on earth God provided this as a home to man, servile and condemned
to exile, and to many living beings, many homes are to be marveled at
in their appearance and opulence [in heaven], which enrapture the eyes
and the soul, with their lovely variegation of colors, gems resembling the
sports of nature, precious metals, gold and silver such as those that exercise
the greed of foolish men, trees laden with apples, nuts, acorns, odorous
herbs, flowers beautiful to the view, birds brilliant with their plumage
and song, animals in their forests and dens, flocks and herds wandering
over the hills, rivers sparkling as gems amid the pleasant verdure of their
banks, palaces conjured by art to vie with the heavens, paintings, statues,
raiment of curious weave and stiff with gold. All of this we may believe
is in paradise, from whence all terrestrial things flow down like drops from
an inexhaustible treasure-house, and where God has willed the palace of
his majesty and of all the blessed to be situated.) (419)

This paradise has its inhabitants, all virtual philosophers, even
though in their earthly lives they might have been rustics. Their
occupation is perpetual colloquies on the most exalted topics; their
social system is collectivistic: *Beati quoque nihil seiunctum ab aliis
habent* ("The blessed will likewise possess nothing separately," 421).
Furthermore they will conform to the pastoral setting and the priv-
ileged life of ease in their natures:

Fingite tantum animo urbem ubi nulli egeni, nulli aegroti, omnes in
aureis vestibus, omnes sapientes, nullae casae paleis constructae et ramal-
ibus, sed aedes singulae regiarum instar. Talis est caelestis patria. . . .

(Imagine a city where there are no needy people, no diseased, but all
in golden apparel, all wise, no hovels made of boughs and straw, but
individual mansions equal to royal *alcázares*. Such is the country of paradise. . . .) (420)

Until Castellionius, the Dean, and Ferrera can begin to partake in this blessedness they can hope to deserve it while pursuing the Devout Life. The devout may enjoy nature in this world, and there is always the infinite consolation that friendship brings. Mariana describes at this point the many friends he has had, a noble list of names, worthy to adorn the existence of any humanist. And besides, there is a compensation for the devout life in the probability of the acquisition of Divine Grace.

Mariana seems to have been unsound in his understanding of the *De auxiliis* controversy, though by and large adhering to the position of his fellow Jesuit Luis de Molina. The origin of sin for our author is human ill-use of divine aids; God does not so much, therefore, permit it. Freewill is correspondingly exalted as a method of obtaining grace. (The ecclesiastical censors blot out many sentences here in all the copies they can find.) Mariana expresses, on the other hand, a feeling of attraction to Augustine's doctrine of the arbitrariness of the gift of grace. (So the censors blot out a whole page here, too.) When Ferrera proposes that this disregard of circumstances by God is rather cruel, Mariana tries to harmonize doctrines and elaborate a notion of two distinct classes of the predestined. (This infuriates the censors, as may be imagined.) The historian's concern to be fair to all reputable sources appears not to be applicable to the niceties of theology, and Mariana's text could indeed have induced more captious souls into heterodoxy.

A final Admonition to the Dying brings to a close this most personal of Mariana's writings on what he thought was the most universal of beliefs, so much so that it must have been suggested to us by nature herself whispering in our ears (*vox naturae nostris insonans auribus*). The piece has never been translated into any modern language, yet it deserves study, both for its demonstration of how the humanistic dialogue could be enlivened by characterization, humor, and curious learning, and for its accord with that persuasion of all essayists: the truth lies hidden; we are played upon by ideas and imaginary things (. . . *veritas latet; spectris et imaginibus ludimur,* 363).

The Debate on Saint James of Spain

The Apostle St. James the Greater is the patron saint of Spain. The battle-cry "Santiago!" had resounded throughout the Reconquista and the wars of the sixteenth century, and appeared to have brought victory to Spanish arms on many occasions. The common belief in Spain was that the apostle had brought Christianity to the country in the first century, so it was vexatious to many when the non-Spanish Cardinal Baronius, in his work on the saints, declared that there was no actual proof of this visit. Some Spanish churchmen were inclined to agree, especially Mariana's friend García de Loaisa, who in 1593 made known a document of a former archbishop of Toledo, Rodrigo, casting doubt already in 1215 on the veracity of records of the apostle's arrival.[9] Mariana, as a historian and a Toledan, was disposed to support Loaisa, though he was aware that the text might have arisen from a medieval polemic in which the stakes were the maintenance of the primatial see of Spain at Toledo or the loss of it to Santiago de Compostela, a rich center of pilgrimages. Rodrigo, that is, might not have been sincere in his claim.

At this point the pedigree-conscious Don Juan Fernández de Velasco, Constable of Castile, and his librarian, Mariana's *bête noire* Pedro Mantuano, challenged him. Their treatise, issued in 1605, impugned Mariana's scholarship and our author began to prepare his reply to all *novi consarcinatores* ("recent cobblers-together of facts"). He was aware of the climate of subterfuge prevalent in his time, particularly as a result of the affair of the lead tablets of Granada;[10] in his manuscript notes he declares his principles: "We adore only what we know to be true" and "Truth is the daughter of time."

The importance Mariana gave to this question is demonstrated by his placing his thirty-page treatise "On the Coming of the Apostle James the Greater to Spain" in first position among his *Tractatus septem* [Seven Treatises, Cologne, 1609] and in his allowing the dedication, to no less a personage than Pope Paul V, itself largely to refer to the matter:

Vetera carcinomata contactu saeviunt amplius, neque se manu aut stylo contrectari sinunt adversa remedia pervicacia: quod supremum miseriae genus est. Quod rei praesentis est tamen, ut quo festinat oratio nostra; lis ante paucos annos exorta est gravissima: venerit B. Iacobus Apostolus Maior in Hispaniam. . . .

(Touching old ulcers makes them spread more widely, and they do not allow themselves to be closed by hand or by lancet [i.e., pen] in the face of the most vigorous remedies. This is the worst kind of misery. For this reason it is an urgent thing at the moment at which our argument is aimed. The dispute that has arisen within the last few years is a very grave one: did St. James the Greater come to Spain?)

The surprising thing is that Mariana here comes around to the Constable's position, and concedes that what evidence there is must persuade a historian of good conscience that the mission really did take place. Though he is a Toledan and a man who holds the now dead Loaisa in fond memory, Mariana shows no *parti-pris;* the documents he has handled have persuaded him. The truth may be otherwise, but it must await more and better texts being brought to light. He had decided to go to sources earlier than Archbishop Rodrigo: Isidore of Seville's *De ortu et obitu patrum* [The Birthplaces and Death-Sites of the Saints]; eighteen ancient breviaries of various churches; the writings of Pope Calixtus II (died 1124); and the section of the *Chronicle of Iria* (c. 984) that tells how King Ramiro II prayed to St. James before his victory over Abderrahman at Simancas.[11] Mariana makes it clear that he will not take on trust what popes may have said on the subject, and most copies of *Seven Treatises* have this phrase heavily scored out by the censor!

This debate did not stop with Mariana's treatise, and has in fact had a lively existence down to our own times. *On the Birthplaces* can be shown to be by another hand than Isidore's (as Baronius had suspected) and to be a text of the eighth century,[12] so that at present a non-Spanish text of c. 650, the "Breviary of the Apostles," which does speak of St. James's Spanish ministry, appears to be what disseminated the legend inside and outside Spain.[13] The other thorny question, that of the original and final resting-places of St. James's remains, also was of concern to Mariana in his treatise.

Against Public Shows: A Brutal but Unsuccessful Attack

There have always existed powerful psychological factors that have inhibited people's appreciation of public spectacles, extending to an aversion to sitting to watch even serious drama, and in freethinkers and pagans as much as in devotees of the great organized religions. The whole phenomenon can be seen by some as subversive of social and emotional order; an early anecdote is that of the reproach of Solon to Thespis: that seeing things performed mimetically on a stage will cause the viewers to want to act out what they have seen in real life. In terms of the Spanish theater, *las burlas* will become *las veras*. [14] The visible has indeed a more direct appeal to the multitude than the merely audible, and censorship of public shows has been widespread in all ages, surviving until very recently in Great Britain, for instance. On the other hand the literary texts of plays and interludes have never caused such concern, have usually escaped censorship as such, and are indeed dismissed as of small consequence for the moralist by St. Thomas Aquinas. [15]

How was it then possible that Mariana, in his treatise *De spectaculis* [On Public Shows], attacked every manifestation of spectacle, putting even poetic drama of high distinction on a level with bullfights and visits to brothels? Has not the drama in Spain ever been a lively composite of popular philosophy, of notions of national history, and of religious vulgarization? To deal with these questions it may be profitable first to survey the attitudes prevailing among ecclesiastical moralists from long before 1609, the date of the treatise.

It appears that before the accession to the throne of Philip II only the apparel of actors had preoccupied the authorities enough to provoke the proclamation of a law, that of Charles I and Juana (1534).

No century in the early modern period has been without religious controversy or without the universal belief that public and private sinfulness would bring about disastrous effects upon the metaphysical and the physical health of societies, even when they did not expressly provoke God into sending natural and military calamities. The instructors of royal confessors and the academic teachers of moral theology had therefore to prepare themselves for discerning and recommending the rooting out of the apparently trivial causes of the sinfulness. Early clerical moralists, and Fray Francisco de Alcocer is an example, had declared in a treatise of 1559 that dancing, performing, and attending theatrical shows *(farsas)* and the wearing of masks were not necessarily sinful, but were a grievous waste of a conscientious Christian's time.[16] Later in Philip II's reign we find theologians and casuists who hold opinions both for and against theatrical performances, and often they took sides in accordance with rivalries between religious orders. The Augustinians tended toward toleration; the Jesuits already toward a unanimity in opposition to the theater. Most attacks were directed against histrionic costume and travesty, the behavior of actors and especially of actresses onstage and in society, and the promiscuity of men and women, persons of quality and the dregs of the commonalty, in the audiences of the *corrales*.

We have already observed Mariana providing his explanation for the terrible naval reverse of 1588:

> Gravium scelerum quae in nostra gente vigent ea vindicta fuit, et nisi animus fallit, cuiusquam principis viri malae libidines divinum numen irritarunt. . . .

> (These things were vengeance for the serious delinquencies that are current among our nation, and unless the mind is deceived, the evil desires of a certain prince enraged the divinity.) *(De rege)*

This kind of diagnosis of the source of the adversities Spain was suffering coincided, as it happened, with the total revolutionizing and formal crystallization of the Spanish theater due to the genius of Lope de Vega. The moral regulation of the newly prosperous theater became a matter of urgency for the moralists, who were additionally conscious of the fact that the *corrales* of their day were maintained to produce a profit for religious charities. A petition for a Canon Law ruling went out from the hospitals in 1589, and the University of Alcalá had to disappoint them by declaring that shows are all sinful, since they inevitably put sin into the mind of the beholder. During the next decade only adverse opinions such as this one seemed to get a hearing. Pedro de Rivadeneira, S.J., began the diatribe against the inclusion of dancing in shows (*On Tribulation*, 1589), while Marco Antonio de Camos, O.S.A., in his *Microcosmia, or the Universal Rule for the Christian Man's Behavior* (Barcelona, 1592; Madrid, 1595) establishes the litany we shall recognize over and over again in Mariana: *nuevas invenciones del demonio, . . . a que llaman zarabanda* ("new inventions of the devil, which they call sarabandes"); *tan lascivos y sucios los meneos y gestos* ("so lustful and filthy [are] the body-movements and gestures"); *tanta soltura y deshonestidad* ("so much license and indecency"); and *danzas y bailes tan abominables* ("abominable dancing and cavorting").[17] Camos does not, however, include plays in his denunciations, and says he will not presume; this, we shall see, is to show more fairness than Mariana.

In 1597 the death of Philip's daughter Doña Catalina, Duchess of Savoy, shut the theaters in mourning and also prompted the aged king to consult the clergy, including Mariana's associate García de Loaisa, on the moral lawfulness of plays and shows of all kinds. The committee reported that they thought such diversions were above all debilitating because of the pleasure they induce, and just as a formal banquet would be cheapened by the provision of dancers, so is the theater cheapened and turned into an indecent occasion.[18] The City Council of Madrid appealed against this document, which threatened to keep the theaters closed from May 2, 1598, indefinitely. They argued that all societies, and many admirable ones, have tolerated the theater. Plays can be didactic, and show virtue and justice in action and being rewarded. Relaxation, they declare in humanistic fashion, improves the spirit of the active man.[19] They avoided the religious arguments, though it was all turned into rather an academic discussion when the king died later in the year. The new king and his favorite the Duke of Lerma were not prejudiced against the theater, and the *corrales* reopened on April 17, 1599.

Before 1609, the date of Mariana's treatise, Lerma had himself consulted the clerical opposition, but even they seemed to realize that the cause of total prohibition was lost. Among the measures promulgated at that time for the theaters were merely the minor ones of limiting the number of companies of players, of separating the sexes in the audience, of excluding members of the clergy at all times, of regulating actresses' attire, and of censorship of plays in the text.[20] A move to exclude women from appearing onstage, as they were excluded in England at that time, was unsuccessful. The enforcing of all these new ordinances was seldom effective, and Cervantes by 1605 is writing that the pleasure principle is paramount in his day, censorship is almost a dead letter, and evil *comedias* are judged so on aesthetic grounds alone. Even a few Jesuits reduced their opposition: Tomás Sánchez, S.J., that polymath of sexual and matrimonial complication, and Luis Alfonso de Carvallo (admittedly *later* a Jesuit), the literary theorist, were both among this carefully treading group. On the other side were writing those correspondents of Mariana, the brothers Leonardo de Argensola, of whom one, Lupercio, was himself a closet dramatist (but also a salaried royal chronicler of Aragon). He wrote a *Memorial,* directed against the theaters of his times, putting into it several scandalous and sometimes ludicrous anecdotes concerning undignified people being allowed to play inappropriate roles in sacred plays, and unscrupulous producers allowing unseemly dances to accompany plays with religious themes.[21] We shall perhaps be tempted to conclude, after reading what Mariana has to say on the subject, that of all the aspects of the theater of his age *this* was the only one he had even read about.

Mariana is indeed entirely unaware of what went on in the public theaters of Spain, and he freely admits it. He has been present at no spectacle of any description, but this does not inhibit in the least the implacability of his treatise's attack. His "On Public Shows" simply ignores the drama or even the interlude of farcical type *(entremés)* that his contemporaries knew and we ourselves know, and recapitulates the descriptions (and the calumnies) of the ancient orators, like Aelius Aristides,[22] and of the Fathers of the Church, like Arnobius, St. John Chrysostom, and Tertullian (whose own *De spectaculis* deals with gladiatorial arena sports).[23] His statement of intention says as much: *Veterum ludorum insaniam nova disputatione* De spectaculis *compescere* ("To restrain the folly of the ancient games by means of a new treatise 'On Public Shows' "). What we read in his work, then, is largely a wealth of Patristic erudition placed at the service of a false analogy: bacchanalian shows are not the standard by which the highly ethical and poetical plays of (frequently clerical) dramatists, and even their studies of the intrigues in love and adventure of high-born ladies and men, ought ever to be judged.[24]

Mariana's hatred of the theater goes much deeper, and this is why he feels the need to perpetuate the confusion throughout his treatise by continually shifting the ground of his argument. Men's interest in plays, he asserts, begins with their curiosity:

> . . . estos hombres [those who despise other trades] por su interés han juntado en uno todas las maneras e invenciones para deleitar el pueblo que se pueden pensar, como cualquiera dellas tenga fuerza para suspender los ánimos de los hombres—porque primeramente se cuentan historias de acaecimientos extraordinarios que se rematan en algún fin y suceso más maravilloso, como lo vemos en las tragedias y comedias: cosas increíbles componerse y afeitarse de manera que no parecen fingidas sino acaecidas y hechas. Y es propio de nuestra naturaleza maravillarnos de cosas extraordinarias y menospreciar lo que pasa cada día.

> (These men have, for their own profit, gathered together all kinds of novelty to amuse the people which can be imagined, of which any single kind is sufficient to enthrall men's minds—because in the first place stories are told of unusual and astonishing events, and these culminate in some even more wonderful ending, as we see happening in tragedies and comedies: incredible things are put together and adorned in such a way that they do not seem to be fictions but real events. And it is part of our nature that we should be astonished at unusual things and scornful of what happens every day.)

From this naive, one might say Quixotic, account of human curiosity in servitude to the marvels of mimesis, Mariana turns to a consideration of men's delight in words, especially the elegances of rhyme and meter, falling back on the old Pythagorean number-mysticism: *porque los que estamos compuestos de números, más que ninguna cosa nos deleitamos con ellos* ("Because, since we are ourselves composed of numbers, we are delighted with them above all other things").[25] He moves from this to the ingenuity of the action, the amenity of the decor and the costumes, and the heady presence of handsome actors and actresses, not to mention the sight of women in the audience, too. Most perilous of all as a stimulus to avid playgoing there are the jokes, the music, the dances, and those supple body movements:

Los movimientos deshonestos de los farsantes, y los meneos y voces tiernas y quebradas con las cuales imitan y ponen delante de los ojos las mujeres deshonestas, sus meneos y melindres, ¿de qué otra cosa sirven sino de encender en lujuria a los hombres, los cuales por sí mismos se son harto inclinados a los vicios?

(The indecent movements of the players and the body-gestures and sweet, falsetto voices with which they imitate and reproduce the actions of obscene women, their agitations and their endearments, what are these but ways of inflaming the lasciviousness of men who are in principle most inclined to vice?)

Mariana can cite horrible cases: a noble youth of Cordoba ran away with a company of players, causing great grief to his family, while a clergyman of Toledo eventually lost his sight from too much watching of *comedias*. If the reader, however, is not exactly put in mind of any notable play of the Spanish Golden Age by the passage that has just been quoted, but perhaps rather of some reported performance of Greek New Comedy that has not survived except in an ancient sermon or a harangue by Aelius Aristides, the true target of Mariana's attack is patent. The deeper matter, what he saw as the deeper evil, was that "fabricator of death," the hedonistic principle itself. Therefore the greater the literary value of the dramatic production, the greater the danger to the souls of its audience. He does not, apparently, concern himself with either the soul of the dramatist (such as his later friend Lope de Vega),[26] or that of the reader of a poetic drama on the page, in his study. On the other hand, even sacred drama, if acted in public, would enjoy no special immunity from this clerical censure; for Mariana it would still have its irremediable affinity with some lewd entertainment in a bawdy-house.

Sixteen of the twenty-five chapters of "On Public Shows" are devoted to acted entertainments; of the others, five are on bullfighting (including the texts of three papal briefs condemning it, all cited in full), two form a general conclusion, while three deal with,

precisely, bawdy-houses. Now Mariana's mentor in the ancient
world, Aelius Aristides, had already compared the singsong delivery
and artful gesticulations of mimes with entertainment supplied by
prostitutes; this is what our author probably is referring to when
he says that he has passed to the subject *por ocasión que se ofreció*
("by a convenient accident"). He is convinced that there is a comparable evil in the two places of resort, although he astonishes us
by his preparedness to defend bawdy-houses as less prejudicial in
the balance of things than public theaters! He has, of course, no
reformer's interest in the women who inhabit them, assuming that
their welfare is sufficiently provided for by the official municipal
contracts awarded to the *padres de la mancebía* ("managers of houses
of prostitution").[27] He idealizes the days of the early Hebrews,
among whom there was as yet no prostitution, but he is resigned
to it in his own age, especially among the lower classes:

. . . debemos convidar a todos a lo mejor y sufrir a los malos y flacos,
hasta tanto que se contentan con cometer pecados menores, los cuales no
perturban la paz de la república, a la cual se ha de mirar principalmente.

(We ought to urge everyone to be good and suffer those who are wicked
and weak, to the point at which they content themselves with committing
minor sins which do not disturb the peace of society, which we ought to
look to above all else.)

Mariana especially deplores the appeal the trade can make to the
uninhibited sensuality of youths recently arrived in some city where
it is flourishing. In this he resumes the parallel he has established
with theatrical shows.

Our author is enormously concerned with the incidental profit
to be made out of prostitution by those not directly engaged in it;
this is an aspect of the moralist's problem. To collect rent for a
building that facilitates assignations and prostitution, he explains,
is an activity in the same category as selling playing-cards, dice, or
cosmetics: the lessor is in effect allowing another person's free will
alone to decide whether he shall sin, and this is an evasion of a
fellow Christian's responsibility. Mariana has to content himself
with hoping that such indirect vendors will be circumspect; they

are not, after all, dealing in actual weapons. Any such house, however, ought to be let at cost, since in any other circumstances the landlord is making a profit from sin.

Bullfighting is another spectacle Mariana hates, though he knows it will be equally impossible to suppress it. This time it is a matter of a spectacle that successive popes have anathematized (he gives the texts), just as they have, with better results, the driving of frightened animals to slaughter as a spectacle. Our author is one of the first of many Spanish writers to hold the national sport in contempt: *¿ Quién no tendrá por hombre perdido y malo al que se deleitare con tal espectáculo?* ("Who will not declare the man who can take delight in such a spectacle to be reprobate and wicked?"). He anticipates the defense that is always made: the bull has a fair chance to kill his tormentor if (though this less frequently happened in Mariana's time) he is on foot. Then, he rejoins, the bloodlust of the mob will turn itself to the celebration of bulls that are champion killers of men. But in the end he gives up. If those who fling themselves at bulls of their own free will choose to kill themselves, perhaps all one can hope for is that the *alcaldes* will take what safety measures they can. It cannot be prohibited once the fiesta has started any more than can drinking iced water and eating melons, both of which things have killed many before now.[28]

To resume this survey of "On Public Shows," one can only speculate what the real, not the ostensible, subject of it is. Given the favorable view taken of the theater in both court and city by 1609, Mariana can have expected little practical result, and indeed there was none. The theater probably gained rather than lost from all the controversies and threats of closure of the beginning of Philip III's reign, and found new ethical and aesthetic purpose.[29] It may also be the case that absolutist governments promoted a theater that did not challenge its positions, and in fact carried their propaganda in the interests of the cohesion of the state.[30] The enemies of the theater, principally Mariana's own Society, went on theorizing antagonistically and awaiting some national disaster that might then be blamed on the sins of Spain's theatergoers and the social dissolution they had contributed to.[31] There is an interesting parallel with "On Public Shows" perhaps, in the treatise against witchcraft

written by King James VI of Scotland (and at that time also James
I of England). A recent study of King James's conceptual world
suggests that what he really was writing against was social disorder,
and found witchcraft a useful topic since it had so many features
antithetical to order. Cosmic and social disorder could be written
of in a language identical to that used in describing witchcraft and
the sabbat.[32] It may well be, therefore, that Mariana assimilated the
description of the most disorderly shows to that of prostitution,
bullfights, and social degeneration in general since he felt a similar
metaphysical horror. His account of the Spanish theater of his time
is so ludicrously inappropriate because it was not his real subject
at all.

The Minor Treatises and "On Alterations in the Value of Currency"

Mariana left, as we have seen, a large quantity of manuscript
notes toward possible future works of erudition; these notes have
come down to us frequently on the reverse sides of old letters to
him, thus preserving them. From them it appears he had an interest
in chemistry. He records a number of chemical recipes: "For the
Stone That Lights Up," "For the [Experiment] of the Ring," and
others, often with the names of certain substances left in Greek. He
also provided a translation of an otherwise unknown Agostino
Gellio's work on bees and silkworms, but neither of these interests
took concrete shape in a treatise or book.[33]

He produced several works of the "aids to study" type. The first
is *De ponderibus et mensuris* [On Weights and Measures], which represents an attempt to give a relative value in terms of Mariana's own
age of the weights and measures mentioned in the Bible and in
Classical authors.[34] There are related treatises on chronology, *"De
annis Arabum"* [On the Islamic Year-Computation] and *"De die mortis
Christi"* [On the Date of Christ's Death], for both of which Mariana
devises pages of tables to accommodate the Christian Era, the Year
from the Hegira, the Jewish Year, and the Era of the Caesars, as
far ahead as 1742. In the companion treatise on the date of the
movable Easter he omits no factor of computation: dominical letters,

epacts, golden numbers, cycles of indiction, solar cycles and lunar cycles, the New Years in both Jewish and Christian calendars, regular and bisextile years, Passover and Easter down to 1997. He fixes the date of the Crucifixion as the eighth day before the kalends of April, that is March 25. This calculation of Good Friday illustrates a perennially thorny problem, which still exercises chronologists. It appears that there was no Passover on a Friday between the years A.D. 27 and 34, while the eve of the Passover *possibly* fell on a Friday in A.D. 30 and in A.D. 33. The dating of the first Good Friday is consequently hard to relate to the Feast of the Passover in the most likely years.[35]

His *"Pro editione vulgata"* [Treatise in Favor of the Vulgate] is a moderate document for that age of scriptural controversy and of the general rejection of Jerome's Latin translation of the bible by Protestants, who favored direct access to the original Hebrew and Greek texts. Our author's position had, nevertheless, been held before by his fellow Jesuit Robert Bellarmine in 1586. The recommendation is that the Vulgate and the other Latin translation of repute, the *Vetus Itala,* must be considered the best obtainable, and should certainly remain unchallenged when texts are appealed to in matters of faith and morals. In minor matters of biblical erudition, the identification of Hebrew antiquities, or research into topography and natural history, for instance, emendations to the Vulgate's text are not unreasonable. This treatise is, then, an ancillary document to Mariana's *Scholia to the Old and New Testaments,* which is not the work of a man of letters and requires no discussion here.

No one, Mariana points out, knows better than a historian that if later ages do not learn from history those errors committed in the past will be repeated. *On Alterations in the Value of Currency* is therefore a treatise full of instances drawn from the historical record, of monarchs who hoped to augment their finances by immoral methods, and above all by refusing to consult with constituent assemblies of those who were to be expected to pay them tribute. The chronicles of the Middle Ages present us with a series of monarchs who chose to give coinage a fictitious superior value, which a decreased content of silver could not sustain commercially; prices of commodities consequently always went up in proportion. The celebrated Gresham's

Law, independently stated by Mariana: *Aeris quando copia nimis est, argentum certe inter cives evanescit et perit* ("When there is an excess of copper coinage silver will certainly disappear and die out among the citizenry"), has been in operation again and again, yet monarchs have proved incapable of being persuaded. Charles VII of France set a bad example, albeit excusable when his kingdom was overrun by his enemies, when he consistently abridged the rights of his subjects' assemblies in matters of deciding on taxation. In the case of Spanish kings there has never existed any equivalent excuse, and in Mariana's own time the king is presented as about to flood the country with base and easily counterfeited *vellón*. A commission ought to have been consulted, although our author concedes that deputies of the people are often incompetents:

. . . porque los más de ellos son poco a propósito, como sacados por suertes, gentes de poco ajobo en todo y que van resueltos a costa del pueblo miserable de henchir sus bolsas; demás que las negociaciones son tales que darán en tierra con los cedros del Líbano.

(Because most of them are of small consequence, being chosen by lot, men of very little initiative in anything and who attend resolved to line their pockets at the expense of the poorest; in addition to this, their deliberations are such that they will always drag themselves out until the cedars of Lebanon fall.)

But in spite of this Mariana is of the opinion that fiscal policy is better left in the hands of these dilatory knaves and fools than in those of the king and his favorites.

His bitterly indignant thirteenth and last chapter is devoted to what happens, at the worst, to the money paid in taxes. Even the Prudent King, Philip II, had lavished huge personal allowances on his legitimate son Don Carlos and his illegitimate half-brother Don Juan, showing his prudence only, according to the view of Mariana, in knowing when to waste no more resources on the doomed territories in the Netherlands. Again, patronage is bestowed by monarchs in no proportion to real merit, and there is no more recent instance than that of king Henry III of Castile of a king personally auditing what has been spent. That monarch had detected what we nowadays would call "cost overruns" in the financing of a project to convert old castles into state prisons, and had immediately made an example of some rapacious treasury officials. Prodigality and mere finery eat up far too much of the rest of the revenues, and at that point every royal official begins to imitate the king, to the nation's loss:

> Yo aseguro que si abriesen esos vientres comedores que sacasen enjundia para remediar gran parte de las necesidades.

(I assure you that if some of those greedy bellies were to be slit open enough fat could be extracted to remedy a good deal of [the people's] neediness.)

More proposals emerge: each official should make a declaration of personal assets before taking office, just as bishops are obliged to do; the Spanish king himself ought to glance occasionally at the way things are arranged in that great realm so idealized by the Jesuits, the Chinese Empire.

The monarch and his advisers were not, it hardly requires saying, ready for this treatise and its admonitions. Sometimes even those who have indeed learned from history are condemned to repeat its discomfitures, and Mariana must have been little surprised when he was arrested within months of publishing his *Seven Treatises*.

Chapter Five

Mariana's Style, Posterity, and Legend

A Distinctive Style of Spanish Prose

If our author has any celebrity today, or indeed survival into the twentieth century, as a man of letters and not as, for instance, a political theorist, it is a consequence of his style. A later dissident Jesuit, Miguel Mir, is able to assert that Mariana is the only writer of the Society, out of the thousand who may have used Latin or Spanish prose, whose style is truly original and of whom one single clause will immediately reveal the individuality.[1] This may well be the infatuation of an admirer of Mariana's subject matter, but there has been over the centuries a willingness on the part of those who value the peculiar energies and elegances of Castilian prose to praise Mariana.

The obligation he was under to translate his *History* from the original Latin, or at least to edit carefully what others may have assisted him to translate, and also to work with a certain speed, may have led to his retention of certain prose constructions which are more effective and more usual in Latin, notably short, analytical sentences, paratactic and economical of clauses introduced by conjunctions.[2] He decides to be very sparing indeed of the gerund as a replacement for the clause at a time when that construction was palpably overused, possibly even by Cervantes and Mateo Alemán.[3] In Spanish versions of his treatises Mariana seems to have felt less of an aesthetic impulse, and allowed these contemporary formal devices to have their effect on a contemporary readership that expected them. This contrasts with the *History,* which, though "artistic" in conception, has a style that is unpretentious and has hardly dated.

The *General History of Spain* contains, as we have seen, many passages in which statesmen and great captains harangue their listeners. It is almost worthy to be used as a manual of oratory for appropriate public occasions. Such passages have, therefore, a certain figurative ostentation, some "impressionistic" omissions of verbs from sentences,[4] and some pairings of adjectives and phrases within longer units of discourse on the Ciceronian model. From the rather pedantic purist Munárriz Mariana wins the accolade of *elegante,* which is explained as "showing an appropriate use of ornateness, and imagination in the choice of his figures of speech".[5]

Dogging the reputation of our author down the years has been the preference he showed in his *General History* for archaic terms. It has often been dismissed as a defect in style; Saavedra Fajardo's jest in his *República literaria* [Literary Commonwealth, 1655] is well known:

Afecta la antigüedad, y como otros se tiñen las barbas por parecer mozos, él por hacerse viejo.

(He affects quaintness, and just as others tint their beards to seem younger, he does so to appear an older man.)

These archaisms are absent from his letters, from his rough copies, and from the translations of his treatises. Obviously these terms were meant to have a literary effect, to convey the flavor and specificity of ancient documents, and sometimes, as Mariana explains in his preface, because there is an irreplaceable correctness in an obsolete term. There is, incidentally, no case of verbal coincidence with the contemporary essays in archaism practiced by Cervantes's Don Quijote, though the intention is, of course, similar—once we concede Don Quijote's fundamentally unsound approach to "the past." Many terms were, moreover, not so obsolete as some commentators have supposed, and one has to bear in mind Mariana's emigration from Spain in 1561: much of the archaism is merely the Spanish of Charles V's reign.[6] After all, the words that "adhere from the pages of chronicles," to use Mariana's expression, do in fact bring with them an aroma of the pastness of the past, a quality which the Romantic novelists like Sir Walter Scott were later to exploit.

The other matter that worried commentators was: is there an adequate thought process to support this unflaggingly elegant style? They knew that Mariana had disclaimed any special originality in the preface, and they could see the banality behind the beautiful cadences of his "moral commentary," and even of the speeches attributed to historical personages. Perhaps we could conclude that it *was* essentially written for a boy prince,[7] and later adapted for *la gente vulgar* ("the common people") as the preface indicates.

Mariana as a Latin Poet

Everything Mariana published in his lifetime was, as we have seen, in Latin. Among his private papers we may find his notes and letters in Castilian, some of which later saw the light of publication. He wrote no Castilian verse, and in his day this was the custom in the Society of Jesus.[8] The few Latin poems he left are, however, of a very high order of their kind.

It is notoriously hard for us in the twentieth century to evolve a critical language in which to discuss the Latin verse of the Renaissance and the following centuries.[9] At its best it is not simply the result of constructing lines of concordant Latin words according to the contemporary rule-books of Latin prosody. Poetic texture is as undeniably present in the best poems as in their Romance congeners. There has existed, however, a twofold prejudice against the consideration of this area of literature: on the one hand a scorn of it by both Classical humanists, who see Renaissance poets at best as epigones, and by appreciators of vernacular poetry, who have been disposed to see in it no more than an unadventurous setting down of merely imitated beautiful form; and on the other a Romantic and post-Romantic denial of any emotional fidelity: the new poets have merely coopted the emotional patterns of Virgil, Horace, Ovid, and the rest instead of looking into their own hearts, according to this view.

The powerful emotional impulses set in motion by the reader's happening upon a word shared by lyric poetry and the language of

heightened moments in his or her emotional life are evidently un-
available in a language that lives in books alone (or, in this particular
case, in lapidary inscriptions); "forlorn!", "nevermore!", and more
modern signal words cannot have Latin counterparts in our age. The
pathetic passages in Renaissance Latin poems are usually echoes or
even transpositions of similar passages of Classical pieces, and the
applause of the critic has often gone to the ingenuity with which
the later poet has set the ancient gem in its new setting.[10] As I
believe will be seen, Mariana is not obviously one of these gem-
setters, but a poet worthier of other applause.

An approach toward the evaluation of the elusive substantiality
of this type of verse has been put forward: the comparison with
painterly works of the same period, where a landscape is populated
with antique figures, giving it an air of relative eternity and mon-
umentality. Petrarch uses the very term: *umbra quaedam et quem
pictores nostri aerem vocant* ("a certain shading and what our painters
call 'atmosphere'"),[11] but he also advocates the minute fragmentation
of the Classical authors' phrases to be relied on to transpose this
"air." (One need hardly remark here that Petrarch himself was soon
to join the ranks of Classical authors, and that subsequent poets
were in their turn incorporated. The task of identifying amid this
new accession of poets as well as amid these of Classical antiquity
the precise sources of Mariana's phraseology may by now be practically an impossible one. One merely surmises that there must have
been poetical models.) Just as the painters' landscapes-with-figures
are artistic unities, so are those Latin poems that incorporate the
relics of their authors' memories of their passionate readings.[12] The
new poems represent the poets' conversations with their models in
previous times. They are also their attempts not to be thought to
have immersed themselves in the ephemeral present alone, at a
moment in history when there was a new consciousness of the ap-
palling voracity of time.

Mariana's verse is less dependent on readings of previous authors
than, in the phrase already in use, contaminated by them. Petrarch
again supplies the principle he must have known: *Utendum . . .
ingenio alieno, utendumque coloribus, abstinendum verbis* ("The other
poet's poetic power may be used, also his rhetorical colors; his actual

words are to be avoided").[13] So there is a recognizable Virgilian gravity and rusticity, contaminating Mariana's two principal poems, an untitled one we might call "The Speaking Grove" in *On Death and Immortality* (358) and his manuscript epicedium *"Ad Castelionum in obitu uxoris et filiae"* [To Castellón on the Deaths of his Wife and Daughter].

The former of these presents the shared pathos of natural objects with the springs of human emotion in the extreme form of allowing those objects of the rural scene to find their own voice.

[The Speaking Grove]
Densas sub salices lassa et confecta, viator,
  Proiice tantisper membra labore viae.
Lucus amoenus eram: quercus, virgulta, cupressos
  Leniter aspirans commovet hic Zephyrus.
Floribus et lucent distincta haec prata decoris
  Vere thymum et violam cum redeunte ferunt.
Atque fragrans inter terebinthos innatat iris;
  Nympharum proprius lucus Amadriadum.
Multaque cum violis vaccinia fusca leguntur,
  Perque humiles dumos roscida mixta rosa est.
Aspice nocte polum, varios hosce aspice flores;
  Quis neget in terris astra micare diu?
Hic ver purpureum laetissima germina fundit;
  Rura salutari spargit odore mea.
Mollior hic aestas; praebet quos pampinus umbras
  Aura fovet leviter frondea testa movens.
Arboribus surgit molli connexa corymbo
  Nigra hedera in pratis non pede recta suo.
Est hic vinetis confusa et pinguis oliva,
  Palladis et Bacchi munera iuncta simul.
Sunt olera irriguis lactuca et beta salubres,
  Agricolis caules, allia, rapa, siser.
Praecipites inter rupes pura unda perennat
  Fonticulo et tenui murmure grata suo.
Rivus item placidus nostras perlabitur oras
  Sylvam humore rigans, quae prope tonsa nitet.
Lusciniaeque modos solitos tum aestate cicada
  Armonia indocili concinit usque melos.
Est et turdus edax, perdix et turtur obesus,

Attagen in mensis saepe petitus honos.
Inque plagas truduntur apri, leporesque fugaces,
Cuniculi imbelles, grata sagina gulae.
Tendimus alitibus laqueos, indagine vulpes
Luditur—heu corti parce inimica meae!
Agresti arbusto sponsatur ab arbore miti
Surculus, ut domino non sua poma ferat.
His amor, hoc pulchris nomen bene convenit hortis
Quando tot veneres hunc tenuere locum.
Villam ne patulam praetergrediaris, amice;
Hospitii facilem nam experiere modum.
Mox oculis lustra quae audisti singula; dices:
—Est, fateor, meritis apta camoena tuis.

(Traveler, spread out for a while those limbs, tired and stiff from the effort of the road, beneath the leafy willows. Once I was a pleasant grove. Here oaks, underwood, cypresses, all are moved by gently wafting Zephyrus. These glades of beauty are variously set off by flowers; they bear the thyme and the viola at his return. The iris, too, swims fragrantly among the terebinths; this grove is the Hamadryads' own. There are gathered many dusky berry-bushes among the violas, while the dew-laden rose is inextricable from the humble briars. At night, observe the pole-star; look at these varied flowers. Who will deny that the stars also shine by day, close to the earth? Here gaudy spring casts abroad its wanton sprigs and sprinkles the countryside with my health-bringing scents. Summer is blander here. The tendril casts its shadow, while the air softly strokes the leafy treetops as it moves. Hanging in a springy cluster, black ivy climbs up the tree-trunks among the glades, held up on another foot than its own. Here also the succulent olive mingles itself among the winestocks, the gifts of Pallas and of Bacchus coming together in one place. There is kale set in rows, lettuce and beet useful for the cultivator, cabbages, garlic, radishes and rampion. Endlessly among the steep outcrops runs pure water, proud of its spring and its faint murmur. Next the placid river flows past our banks, watering the newly polled copse flourishing close at hand. Now it is summer, the cicada sings its ditties everywhere with untaught harmony, counterpointing the accustomed tunes of the nightingale. Here too lives the voracious thrush, the partridge and the plump turtledove, the wood-cock, that bird often sought as a prize for tables. Into the glades are driven wild boars, evasive hares, timid rabbits, an esteemed tidbit for gluttony. We stretch snares for birds, while the fox is frustrated by the woodman's nets. (Alas! Spare my farmyard, o my enemy!) The twig taken from the fruit-bearing tree is wedded to the wild tree, so that she will bear to her lord apples not her own. Here love is; this name is well fitted to beautiful orchards when so many loves have filled this place. Friend, do not leave behind this spreading plot, since you have enjoyed the easeful song of its shelter. Soon you will survey with your eyes the several things you have been listening to. You will declare: "There is, I insist, a Muse befitting your excellences.") (*De morte,* 358)

This is, of course, descriptive poetry not unlike that of Góngora's *Soledades,* a work that was to appear in the next decade. In both poems there is a passive spectator, or traveler; in Mariana's poem the natural scene itself is feigned as eliciting a muse-inspired work of praise from him. Natural phenomena are, so far as is possible, made anthropomorphic: zephyrs, ivy, brooks, fruit-trees. The profusion of nature is evoked by lists;[14] the planlessness of the poet's description reinforces his contention that he is imitating in words the prodigal enactments of nature herself, of creation itself.[15] Is Mariana a "sincere" poet here? Had he in fact a "feeling for nature"? Probably only in the lines which underscore the economic benefits of nature's foison.[16] We know that the Jesuit training included the fashioning of pastoral and rural imitations of Virgil and Neo-Latin poets; this is an example, albeit an interesting and original one, of what was demanded.[17]

> AD CASTELIONIUM IN OBITU UXORIS ET FILIAE
> Occidit heu coniux tibi luce iucundior omni,
> Post partum proles, proh scelus atque nefas.
> Hic miser, hic flendum, sylvas quoque questubus imple;
> Audiat et gemitus Villaminaia tuos.
> Non vites fallunt, aedesve arsere superbae, venustae,
> Nec census periit, parta labore quies;
> Candida sed coniux vita tibi dulcior ipsa,
> Iuncta parenti infans, vulnera quanta simul!
> Mors, quae cornicibus tot frustra tempora parcis,
> Vatem cur gemino funere saeva petis?
> Gratia pudori iuncta atque utrique venustas
> Extinctae corpus composuere rogo.
> Verum impone modum lachrymis, impone dolori;
> Parcae umbras gemitu sollicitare pio.

An gemitu credis flecti crudelia regna?
Immitis Pluto est, Parcaque saeva furit;
Nempe hominum quisquam coelestia scita vestigat?
Mortales mirum si periere quid est?
Hanc rapit in cunis, illam in flore iuventae;
Increpat aetatis plurima damna senex.
Sic superi voluere; feras quod ferre necesse est.
Concedat fatis Iuppiter ipse suis,
Et populi et gentes, turres, firmissima templa,
Sceptraque de coeli culmine tacta cadunt.
Nos miseri quaerimus, qui ingressi sorte caduca
Non alia vitam conditione sumus.
Defunctos nimio laedi moerore suorum
Crediderim et lachrymis; ergo facesse, dolor.
Elysias choreas plaudunt, aevoque securae
Vivere te laetum, Castelione, iubent.

(Alas, the wife who was more delightful to you than light itself is dead. The infant daughter, too, just after she was born. Oh woe and unhappiness! Here, unhappy man, here there is cause for grief; fill the deep woods with your lament. May Villaminaya also hear your plaints. The vines do not fail, nor have your proud and elegant buildings burned, nor has your crop perished, the meed that labor confers on you—but rather that blameless wife, sweeter to you than life itself, and together with the mother, the child; how many blows at one time! Death, you who spare the crows so many times to no purpose, why do you ruthlessly visit the poet with this double calamity? Grace, accompanied by modesty, and with both of these beauty, have laid the body of the dead lady on the pyre. Allow its true limits to grief, their limit to tears, and beseech the shadowy Fates with a pious lament. But do you believe those cruel regions can be swayed by weeping? Pluto is ruthless; the Fates rage mercilessly. Did any of the race of men ever comprehend heaven's prescriptions? Is it so remarkable that mortals should perish? Death took away the child in her cradle, the lady in the flower of her youth, while this old man complains against the many vexations of age. So the gods have willed it; you will bear what has to be borne. Jupiter himself will obey his own dictates: peoples and nations, towers, solidly built temples, scepters, all must fall when they are touched by a force from above. We wretches who have entered the world subject to transitory chance desire a life under no other condition. I would have believed that the departed were hurt by overmuch mourning and tears shed for them. Therefore, begone grief! They now contemplate the dances of

Elysium, secure from age. They bid you, Castellón, to live more cheerfully.)
(MS Egerton 1875)

There is a certain power to this epicedium, though we may not
know why Mariana selected the curious and discordant image of the
crows as the counterpart of the unhappy widower. [18] The whole piece
allows the poet to employ the commonplaces of Stoicism, a doctrine
he admits in his *General History* (Book 20, chapter 16) has a great
attraction for him. [19] Mariana's other poetic efforts are either translations of Greek epigrams, sometimes moral, sometimes Bacchic,
or poems of circumstance (in unfinished condition among his rough
notes) celebrating activities of fellow members of the Toledo house.
His two short verse attempts at a "curriculum vitae," and his verse
diatribe against Mantuano have already been noticed.

Mariana's Posterity

The accession of Mariana's Latin *Historia* to the University Library
at Salamanca in 1596 was the occasion of the first enthusiastic
encomium of our author. It was given by the humanist Francisco
Sánchez de las Brozas, and this was probably unfortunate in the long
run for Mariana, since that professor was to die four years later in
an odor of heresy, after a life spent imprudently in lay theological
speculation. [20] After the appearance of the Latin treatises there were
to be more adulatory verses, of conventional cast, by the Hellenist
Vicente Mariner. [21] And that was to be practically all. The reputation
of the Jesuit in his native land was effectively in eclipse, and the
impudent tagging he had to suffer in life of being an *afrancesado*
(sympathizer with France) survived him, as we have seen.

On the King and His Education gave Mariana, nevertheless, a durable
celebrity, in both Catholic lands (where it was to diminish) and in
Protestant kingdoms (where it was, if anything, to augment). In
Spain, in such a popularized study of tyrannicide as Lope de Vega's
drama *Fuenteovejuna* (c. 1613), the oppressed villagers of Fuenteovejuna are depicted as potentially tyrannical also; public disorder
is, the viewer of the play might infer, more a motive for terror than
the actions of a tyrant. [22] On the other hand the regicide Bellido
Dolfos in Guillén de Castro's drama *Las mocedades del Cid* [The Early

Years of the Cid, 1614] speaks of the "divine inspiration" he believes
has impelled him to assassinate King Sancho, and this is not exactly
the killing of a tyrant.[23] Mariana's refusal to countenance the doctrine of the Divine Right of Kings placed him outside the purview
of all theorists of the royal prerogative in England and of later
legitimism in France. He had, like all the Jesuits, stressed the purely
utilitarian nature of the kingly office, in order to combat Anglican
and Gallican claims to regal spiritual headship, and the years of the
Great Rebellion in England were a moment in which Mariana's
thought came to be tested. Anglicans in their polemics began to
refer to their enemies as "Jesuits in disguise," and it is true that
Cromwell and other planners of a new kind of state did consult our
author's works. The Royalist Twysden complained that Mariana's
book "is everywhere"; the Parliamentarians Prynne and Rutherford
quoted him (and this led to Rutherford's book being ceremonially
burned twice after the Restoration, in Edinburgh in 1660 and at
Oxford in 1683).[24] The unworldly Puritan minister John Saltmarsh
does not quote Mariana, but captures his spirit in his book of political
aphorisms *The Practice of Policie in a Christian Life* (1639).[25] Theories
of constitutionalism and the right to resistance, which were effectual
in precipitating the English Glorious Revolution of 1688, usually
regarded as summed up in John Locke's *Second Treatise* of 1683,
probably derive from a mass of postmedieval writings, among them
those of the essentially unoriginal Mariana. Republicanism in the
next century had everything to gain from the thought in Mariana's
treatise on the monarch; perhaps it is true that he provided the blade
the Jacobins whetted and used.[26]

The *General History of Spain* had a long career as an agent fashioning
the Spanish consciousness of the country's past, indeed up to the
time of the Peninsular War and beyond. Mariana's synthesis of other
historians' judgments was received uncritically for the most part
until an awareness of the new historiography of "what actually happened," associated with the name of Leopold von Ranke, supervened
in the nineteenth century. Not only the general Spanish reader's
notions of his own country's past were so affected, but also those
of the past of the Indies, which Mariana had taken over from so
early and likewise derivative a source as López de Gómara.[27]

The Spanish style of the *General History of Spain,* with its unmistakable combination of simplicity and austere magnificence,
could not but achieve the praise of posterity. The influential purist
Munárriz, in his adaptation to Spanish of Hugh Blair's Scottish
Enlightenment prescriptions for clarity and figurative economy
above all else, helped to canonize the prose of Mariana, leaving to
one side its deplored archaisms, as worthy to stand beside that of
Cervantes as a model to be emulated.[28]

One could hardly say that the writings of Mariana are much read
in our own day. Every so often a political movement will throw up
a publicist (like the nineteenth-century Liberal Pi y Margall or the
twentieth-century Falangist Ballesteros)[29] intent upon claiming the
Jesuit as his precursor. This normally results in the publication of
rebuttals by political opponents. One can only conclude that the
world has grown older over the intervening centuries; at least secularization in every sphere of moral and political conduct has made
Mariana's promptings entirely irrelevant.[30]

Mariana's Legend

In the centuries following Mariana's death the Jesuits were on the
whole disinclined to consider his reputation favorably, though the
conventional eulogy of how he had been in life, as we have seen,
adorned the pages of their official histories. It was the article on
him by the skeptic Pierre Bayle in his *Dictionnaire historique et critique*
(1697) that contributed most to the spread of Mariana's celebrity
as a writer of good will and integrity. Bayle is not only thinking,
in this article, of Mariana's meticulous habits of scholarship and
refusal of a facile *parti-pris,* but also of his patriotism. He reports
the praise given to this aspect of Mariana's work by René Rapin in
his *Réflexions:* the historian has a never-failing spirit of grandeur to
impart to his native land and its historical vicissitudes (though one
might surmise that Rapin has given too much weight to the sim-
plistic philosophical dicta that punctuate the *General History*). Bayle
reports also the high regard the *History* is in his day acquiring among
Protestants, and how the refugee Mademoiselle de La Roche is (1694)
preparing an abridgment for the English reading public.[31]

A curious result of this appreciation of Mariana in Protestant Europe is an anonymous novel published in Berlin in 1804, *Juan de Mariana, oder die Entwickelungsgeschichte eines Jesuiten* [Juan de Mariana, or the Story of a Jesuit's Adolescence]. Its form is that of an autobiographical fragment "for the eyes of posterity," another *Bildungsroman* of the age. Here Mariana is the son of a layman, a prominent Comunero of Talavera. He becomes a Jesuit novice, but is destined to fall in love with a girl called Inesilla, after hearing her sing first a *romance viejo* and then an ode by Fray Luis de León! Inesilla turns out to be Juan's own sister, and on learning the fact she dies. The rest of the book concerns Juan's reflections on a variety of topics before continuing with his career as a forever saddened and disillusioned Jesuit. This simple tale is adorned with landscape descriptions adapted from those in *On the King and His Education,* but it could not be mistaken for a sixteenth-century piece. German, Romantic, and Protestant sentiments intrude here and there; Juan reflects on a typical problem discerned by men of the Aufklärung— Lavater, or the Goethe of the *Elective Affinities*—why are there such variations in the mental dispositions of members of a single family? The author has probably read Florian's *Gonzalve de Cordoue* (1791) and perhaps also the more ancient *Abindarráez y Jarifa* (c. 1550, but often translated into German), which he has "reversed." Cirot suggests he may be the miscellaneous writer (frequently on Spanish topics) Friedrich Buchholz (1768–1843).[32]

Chapter Six
Conclusion

Mariana must perhaps be considered, within the company of men of letters produced by the Society of Jesus, as one who survived from the order's primitive, more "heroic" era. He inclined more toward a high evaluation of the order's educational mission, and correspondingly less toward appreciating its assumed semipolitical role, that of providing confessors to heads of states. His personal disillusionment with Jesuit politics shows in his pamphlet, never repudiated by him, on the Society's errors in administration. The dilution of the apostolic mission of the order, which he chose to see in his age, and such practices as statutory delation ("syndications") were all unpardonable.

Decisive in the elaboration of Mariana's "alien view" of the Spain of his age was his period of residence in France.[1] His immediate experience of the malfunction of political forces within a potentially invincible and prosperous kingdom obviously remained with him. An irresponsible aristocracy, for whom war was politically profitable, and sectaries of every stripe who would tear the kingdom apart and corrupt the monarch himself to achieve their ends were phenomena that Mariana learned to abhor ever afterwards. The critics who accused him of adopting "French" attitudes in his books were, in spite of their silliness, partly right: the French political system was indeed to be borne in mind, if only because it exhibited so many instances of vices to be avoided. On Mariana's return from France he was no doubt a student of the ways of Philip II's monarchy at its best, in the activities of the subservient royal secretaries Antonio Pérez and Vázquez de Leca, working with the Councils of State. All would be changed in the new reign into which Mariana lived, when the *validos* came into ascendancy and brought about, or were a symptom of, the "crisis of the monarchy." Mariana's invincible opposition to all of those who gained advantage from this crisis—despoilers of the coinage, vainglorious favorites, overreaching confessors—brought him in his lifetime only enmity and imprisonment. Posthumously this opposition helped to confer on him a reputation for decency in a very dishonest time.

As the author of the *General History of Spain* Mariana worked within a tradition. Whereas Morales and Zurita had shown themselves to be truly professional historians, Mariana contented himself with being one of many European Renaissance historians who "put into stylish Latin what others had accumulated." Like the other Renaissance historians he made his work ornate with harangues and set-piece portraiture, of great men and of cities, and instructive with moral positions taken up and conveyed through unremitting eloquence. The predominant model for all of this was Livy, that classical illustrator of the abstract virtues and magnanimity in action. Mariana is extraordinarily judicious in the matter of legendary material, and accommodating to an unwise degree when it comes to the politically charged question of the *falsos cronicones*. This caused the long altercation with the fame-hungry Pedro Mantuano, who willfully disregarded Mariana's carefully stated arguments for leaving some legendary material in the *History*. But after Tamayo de Vargas's loyal defense, Mariana's work of vulgarization could not but gain in popularity.

The *General History* has some resemblances on the ideological plane to *On the King and His Training*, but there is a tendency on Mariana's part to show a pragmatist's interest in history's successful monarchs, and a diminished regard for the place of laws and institutions in shaping Spain's past. His preference is for the principle of combativeness as a motor of history, and beyond that for a providentialist overview. To perfect the Reconquista the individual kingdoms of medieval Spain had their roles to play, but once they were annexed to Castile their importance was over. They became lost within a predestined unitary state.

In producing this immense work Mariana strove above all to say something well, in Latin and in Spanish.[2] It came just too late for its author to avoid the scorn of certain readers who were already half inclined toward a more exact historiography, in preference to edifying and moralized legends. The overall beauty of the work's execution, however, and the unconcealed contempt one finds in it for historical personages whom mere fortune had at some time exalted in the state, ensured that it would have a posterity of admirers. With its series of continuations, postdating Mariana's own last labors on it, the *General History* became the accepted historical record. Even today a handsome reprinting of the work would not be a hopelessly anachronistic project; as in the pages of Edward Gibbon, many would find there a satisfaction in the unfailing style.

The theory and practice of absolutism were to assume the role of innovation in political affairs during the rest of the seventeenth century, while Mariana's version of constitutionalism, with its basis in the imagined primordial civil society of man, was to take on the semblance of mere utopian writing, looking back as it did to a golden age when there existed a wise and powerful Cortes in the Spanish medieval past.[3] This constitutionalism is to be found in *On the King and His Training,* the beginning of which may astonish the reader in that it omits from the story of man's origins the biblical account of Eden and the Fall. Monarchy in those remote times came about, according to Mariana, by popular designation of the best and the wisest, with the assistance of God's providence, but not by any direct conferral of Divine Right. When he considers what has become of the monarchical power in his own times Mariana insists that it must be tempered, even to the extent of allowing the powers of the ancient *ephoroi* of Sparta to the bishops, so odious does he find the influence of ambitious favorites to be. When monarchical powers are exceeded Mariana counsels tyrannicide in the final instance, but his opinions on this extreme measure are purely conventional; it is only the chance sequels of the Ravaillac affair that have, over the centuries, caused *On the King* to be thought of as unique or as an incitement to regicide.

Mariana gives the state no really juridical basis; cohesion comes for him from the strength of its religious, military, and economic bonds. In all of these areas our author is yet another *arbitrista* ("projector"), proposing advances in the appropriate spheres of government. The monarch, he believes, ought to promote religious unity in his realm, for social happiness if for no more immediate reason. This is almost an enlightened attitude to have for that age, though Mariana stops short of advocating actual toleration. Finally, our author is no royalist theoretician; he removes all mystery from the holder of the office of king, and the latter becomes "the chief among civil servants" (as Frederick II of Prussia occasionally liked to style himself).

He was not prescient. The doctrine of the Divine Right of Kings was to prove difficult to do away with, as the progress of secularization caused all religious underpinnings of bodies politic to fall away.[4] The nascent constitutionalism of seventeenth-century Europe became irremediably coupled with man-made bodies of law, and Mariana was temperamentally incapable of seeing possibilities of human happiness in this. His political aphorisms, as we may detach them from his treatises and his *History,* are simply not acute enough when set beside those of, for instance, his contemporaries Antonio Pérez and Giovanni Botero.

Of his *Seven Treatises* the most notorious is his "On Public Shows." In spite of what this treatise promises to study there is no attention paid at all to the developed theater of Mariana's own times. What is more, he constantly confuses the issue, in his implacable hostility to the cultural phenomenon of public shows, for some unstated reason, but possibly because he sensed some perturbation of metaphysical order whenever they took place. Bullfights and visits to brothels, in view of the primary appeal they made to the common man, were for Mariana less of a moral hazard to the Christian than theaters.

In "On Death and Immortality" he might have, given a little more originality of mental cast, made his mark as an essayist. But he lacks that essential willingness of the essayist to abandon authorities. His work is in short a vehicle of the great humanistic Latinizing tradition, with all its close links to a pedagogical endeavor. His strength lies in his unremittingly polished and exact style, behind every clause of which stand the pedagogical precepts of his Society's *Ratio studiorum.*

Notes and References

Chapter One

1. G. Cirot, *Mariana historien* (Bordeaux, 1904), p. 313.
2. Mariana, *Historia general de España,* Book IV (Toledo, 1601) chapters xiii–xiv.
3. María del Carmen González Muñoz, *La población de Talavera de la Reina. Siglos XVI–XX* (Toledo: Diputación Provincial, 1974), p. 418.
4. Ibid., pp. 181–82.
5. G. Cirot, "La famille de Juan de Mariana," *Bulletin hispanique* 6 (1904):310. Another interesting account of the social aspects of Talavera is given by Stephen Gilman, *The Spain of Fernando de Rojas* (Princeton, N.J.: Princeton University Press, 1972), especially "La ynsigne villa de Talavera," pp. 400–16.
6. G. Cirot, "Mariana jésuite. La jeunesse," *Bulletin hispanique* 38 (1936):298.
7. Some astonishing instances of sexual unruliness among Spanish clerics in high places are described in A. W. Lovett, *Philip II and Mateo Vázquez de Leca. The Government of Spain. 1572–92* (Geneva: Droz, 1977), pp. 165–69.
8. E. Michael Gerli, *Alfonso Martínez de Toledo* (Boston: Twayne, 1976), p. 21.
9. Cirot, *Mariana historien,* p. 2, gives the anecdote piously reported by the Jesuit chronicler Andrade in his *Varones ilustres de la Compañía*: Mariana was alone able to pacify a convent of French nuns, thrown into confusion by the actions of one noble nun. He was able to reduce her to obedience again, but we do not learn how he did it.
10. Cirot, "La famille," p. 329.
11. Ibid., p. 321.
12. This controversy is discussed by González Muñoz, pp. 41–43.
13. Mariana, at the beginning of *On the King,* makes much of a Roman votive tablet discovered there with the inscription "L. Vibius Priscus to Togoti." He supposes that the grove was once sacred to Diana, and that Togoti represents a corruption of Toxoti (to the Arrow-Bearer). Since *tagant* means "forest" in many Berber dialects, however, this tablet may not be

dedicated to a Roman's Diana but to a North African's forest numen. On the possible survival of pagan goddess-worship in the region of Talavera, cf. Gilman, citing Andrés de Torrejón (1595), p. 409.

14. Cirot, "La famille," pp. 330–31.

15. Félix Asensio, S.J., "El profesorado de Juan de Mariana y su influjo en la vida del escritor," *Hispania* [Madrid] 13 (1953):581–639.

16. Ibid., p. 585.

17. Ibid., p. 593.

18. Ibid., p. 600.

19. Cirot, "Mariana. La jeunesse," p. 331.

20. Ibid., p. 332.

21. Ibid., p. 334.

22. The first of these autobiographical epigrams is in the Mainz (1605) edition of his *Historia de rebus Hispaniae* (and reprinted in Noguera's edition); the second, in the preface to *Scholia to Both Testaments* (Madrid: Luis Sánchez, 1619).

23. Models for this had been thought out by the leaders of the Comuneros of the early sixteenth century, but their revolt was broken by Charles V just before Mariana's birth.

24. For Mariana's own views on Old Christians and New Christians, cf. his *parecer*, analyzed at the end of the chapter.

25. Mariana shared this interest in sports, apparently. We shall observe him giving great attention both to team games and to games of skill in *On Death and Immortality*.

26. Cirot, "Mariana. La jeunesse," pp. 308–309.

27. Ibid., p. 321.

28. For an analysis by a later Spanish dissident Jesuit of the feasibility of this reform, cf. Miguel Mir, *Historia interna documentada de la Compañía de Jesús* (Madrid: Ratés Martín, 1913), 2:672.

29. Cirot, "Mariana. La jeunesse," p. 348.

30. Cirot, *Mariana historien*, pp. 323–25. The texts are in the British Library Egerton MSS.

31. Cirot, "La famille," p. 326. *Absit omen!*, we may be tempted to think when we bear in mind Mariana's later altercations with another bearer of this surname.

32. Cirot, "Quelques lettres de Mariana et nouveaux documents sur son procès," *Bulletin hispanique* 19 (1917):7–10.

33. On Toledo's decline, cf. David Ringrose, "The Impact of a New Capital City. Madrid, Toledo and New Castile, 1560–1660," *Journal of Economic History* 33 (1973):761–91.

34. Cirot, "Quelques lettres," p. 16.

35. Ibid.

36. Ibid., pp. 21–22.

37. Cirot, "À propos du *'De rege,'* " des *Septem tractatus* de Mariana et de son ou ses procès," *Bulletin hispanique* 10 (1908):98–99.

38. Cirot, *Mariana historien*, p. 120.

39. Lope de Vega, *Epistolario*, ed. Agustín G. de Amezúa. (Madrid: Aldus, 1943), 4:279–80. In another letter, of mid-March 1620, to Eugenio de Narbona, Sessa has Lope explain that he would like to act "as a secular bishop." This may be an echo of Mariana's idea (and that of the early Jesuit general Laínez before him) of the value of episcopal government as a model.

40. Cirot, "Quelques lettres," p. 7.

41. Cirot, *Mariana historien*, p. 126.

42. Cirot, "Les portraits du P. Juan de Mariana," *Bulletin hispanique* 6 (1904):409–11.

43. Cirot, "Quelques lettres," p. 6.

44. Mariana, " 'Respuesta' [to a letter of Bartolomé Leonardo de Argensola], *apud* Juan Antonio Pellicer y Saforcada," *Ensayo de una biblioteca de traductores españoles* (Madrid, 1778), pp. 59–62.

45. Pierre Bayle, *Dictionaire historique et critique*. Fourth edition (Amsterdam and Leiden: P. Brunel, 1730), 3:327–33. On Mariana's chastity, see p. 327, note C.

46. The fact that Mariana is called Royal Chronicler in the title need not imply that it dates from after Philip IV's conferring that rank in 1623. The copyist of the manuscript (Madrid, Biblioteca Nacional 2803, fols. 191v–198r) may have been working at a later date and Mariana may have issued his *parecer* much earlier in his career.

47. Though pointing out that the nobility forms no part of his subject in this paper Mariana shows he is aware of their doubtful claims to Old Christian status: so many, out of interest, intermarried with New Christians "staining not a little through this nasty admixture the cleanness of their ancestry" (*"manchando no poco con esta ruin mezcla la limpieça de su descendencia"*). On the possible inauthenticity of the attribution of the work (consulted in another copy at the Biblioteca Nacional) cf. Albert A. Sicroff, *Les Controverses des statuts de "pureté de sang" en Espagne du XVe au XVIIe siècle.* (Paris: Didier, 1960), pp. 242–43. The notion of the ratio between effort expended in the Reconquista and the loftiness of subsequent ennoblement does, however, occur in *On the King* also; this would argue for the text being genuinely Mariana's.

48. Mariana is emphatically an opponent of attempts at forcible Christianization of Jews. His reference (*Historia general,* Book 26, chapter 13) deserves quotation:

En lo de los judíos hubo mayor dificultad, porque el Rey poco después acordó que les quitasen los hijos de catorce años abajo y que los bautizasen por fuerza—resolución extraordinaria y que no concordaba con las leyes y costumbres cristianas. ¿Quieres tú hacer a los hombres por fuerza cristianos? ¿Pretendes quitarles la libertad que Dios les dio? No es razón, y tampoco que para esto quiten los hijos a sus padres. Sin embargo, los malos tratamientos que hicieron a los demás fueron de tal suerte que era lo mismo que forzarlos. Y aun así se tiene comunmente que la conversión de los judíos de Portugal tuvo mucho de violenta. . . .

(In the matter of the Jews there was more difficulty, because the King shortly afterwards decreed that they should be deprived of all their children beneath the age of fourteen and that these should be forcibly baptized, an extraordinary decision and against Christian law and custom. Do you think men can be made Christians by force? Do you arrogate to yourself the power of removing the freewill which God gave them? It is unreasonable, and equally so to take away children from their parents. However, the ill-treatment that was meted out to all the adults was such that it added up to forcible conversion. In any case it is the general belief that the conversion of the Jews of Portugal had many violent aspects.)

Chapter Two

1. Felix Gilbert, "The Renaissance Interest in History," *apud* Charles Singleton, ed. *Art, Science and History in the Renaissance* (Baltimore: Johns Hopkins University Press, 1967) p. 373.
2. Ibid., p. 376.
3. Nancy S. Struever, *The Language of History in the Renaissance. Rhetoric and Historical Consciousness in Florentine Humanism* (Princeton, N.J.: Princeton University Press, 1970), p. 77.
4. T. J. Luce, *Livy. The Composition of His History.* (Princeton, N.J.: Princeton University Press, 1977), p. xvii.
5. Beatrice Reynolds, "Shifting Currents in Historical Criticism," *Journal of the History of Ideas* 14 (1953): 482–84. Another figure who should not be omitted from a survey of historiographical writing before Mariana is Giovanni Antonio Viperano (c. 1530–1610), a native of Messina who passed through the Society of Jesus between 1549 and 1568, later to become Court Historian in Madrid and finally Bishop of Giovinazzo. His theoretical work is *De scribenda historia* [On Writing History] (Antwerp: Plantin, 1569). For Viperano annals and chronicles are not history; the

latter is only that heightened and clarified narrative which teaches the reader how to act in the future, and what is realizable. If the historian praises or blames this is not tendentiousness, but a wish to steer the reader toward a new consideration of his own future actions, imitation or abhorrence. Later historical successes and failures may be measured against those of the past, and what is more, the incidents of history are a "school of feeling." The rhetorical presentation has its place in the bringing to light of the hidden values of history-as-process from the inchoate darkness of annals. The historian's rhetoric obeys a decorum, related to the prudence and judgment acquired by the man of much experience. This approximates to objectivity; the true historian will be a superior man, generally free from frailties and fears, the *vir bonus,* or Stoic *sapiens* writing presumably for similar *sapientes.* Viperano presupposes a convergence of moral philosophy (which speaks of universals) and history (which records instances), and for this reason the examples of history are so instructive. Viperano also tends toward a cyclical view, e.g., "Men have been through it before; men will go through it again." On this marginally Spanish and Jesuit personage, cf. Eckhard Kessler, *Theoretiker humanistischer Geschichtsschreibung* (Munich: Fink, 1971), pp. 17–21, 36–45.

6. Cirot, *Mariana historien,* p. 144.

7. On earlier historians and their varying credulities, see Eduard Fueter, *Geschichte der neueren Historiographie* (Third edition, 1936, reprinted New York: Johnson, 1968), pp. 222–42. On Florián de Ocampo, see p. 224. He points out that early historians of Germany and Scotland also sought to enhance pre-Christian, non-Roman "prehistories," p. 222.

8. Cirot, *Mariana historien,* p. 135.

9. Ibid., pp. 139–40.

10. Ibid., p. 142.

11. Ibid., p. 153.

12. Mariana, "Respuesta," p. 60. Also Cirot, *Mariana historien,* p. 165.

13. On the question of selection among medieval historians, see Marie Schulz, *Die Lehre von der historischen Methode bei den Geschichtschreibern des Mittelalters* (Berlin and Leipzig: Rothschild, 1909), p. 74.

14. Cited by Marie-Thérèse Hipp, *Mythes et réalités. Enquête sur le roman et les mémoires. 1660–1700* (Paris: Klincksieck, 1976), p. 140.

15. Cirot, *Mariana historien,* p. 334.

16. Ibid., p. 333.

17. Fueter, p. 226.

18. The interest in history as a branch of literature has not ceased to exist in our own times, however. It is susceptible to literary criticism just as the other "imaginative" genres are, and the critic scrutinizes the text

to see how the individual historian has "turned his predicament into opportunity," according to David Levin: "David Levin on 'The Literary Criticism of History,' " *Clio* 1 (1971):42–45. He lists on p. 44 a series of criteria for the understanding of the art of history:

"What principle of order does the historian find in his materials that can allow him to relate one episode, one time, with another? What principles of form does he adopt to express that perception? How does he define, and by what technique does he portray, "the People," or large groups of people? How, in both quotation and paraphrase, does he use the language of his sources?

How does he select details for the portrayal of character? From what point of view—that is, technically from what position—does he describe events? How does he introduce conjecture, and how does he distinguish between conjecture and what he considers documented fact? How does he manage to arrange the events so that those he considers most important appear actually to be the most important events?

How does he move from individual evidence to general judgment, and what relationship does he establish between the typical character or incident and the larger reality that it represents?"

19. Z. García Villada, "El P. Juan de Mariana historiador," *Razón y fe* 69 (1924):456.
20. Cirot, *Mariana historien,* p. 343.
21. Ibid., p. 335.
22. Fueter, p. 226.
23. Gilbert, p. 376.
24. Hipp, p. 145.
25. Gilbert, pp. 382–83.
26. Ibid., p. 389.
27. Ibid., p. 380.
28. Ibid., p. 383.
29. Struever, pp. 62–63.
30. Peter Burke, "A Survey of the Popularity of Ancient Historians. 1450–1700." *History and Theory* 5 (1966):141.
31. Luce, pp. xvi, 139.
32. Ibid., p. 156.
33. Ibid., p. xx.
34. Ibid., p. 231.
35. Ibid., p. 230.

36. Josef Luis Munárriz, *Lecciones sobre la retórica y las bellas artes, por Hugo Blair. Las tradujo del inglés don J. L. M.*, 2nd Ed. (Madrid: Imprenta Real, 1804), 3:256.

37. Paul Merritt Bastett, "The Use of History in the *Chronicon* of Isidore of Seville," *History and Theory* 15 (1976):290.

38. Fueter, p. 226.

39. Sir Philip Sidney's words, at the beginning of Section 7 of his *Defense of Poesy* (1595), cited in Denys Hay, *Annalists and Historians. Western Historiography from the Eighth to the Eighteenth Centuries* (London: Methuen, 1977).

40. Mariana himself avails himself of this commonplace in Book 1, Chapter 7 of his *General History:* Los que describen regiones no conocidas . . . ponen y pintan en aquellas sus cartas o mapas para deleite de los que miran varias figuras de peces, fieras y aves, hábitos extraños de hombres, rostros y visajes extravagantes. Lo cual hacen con tanto mayor seguridad que saben que no hay quien pueda convencerlos de mentira. Lo mismo me parece ha acontecido a muchos historiadores, . . . que donde faltaba la luz de la historia y la ignorancia de la antigüedad ponía uno como velo a los ojos para no saber cosas tan viejas y olvidadas, ellos con deseo de ilustrar y ennoblecer las gentes cuyos hechos escribían y para mayor gracia de su escritura, y más en particular por no dejar interpolado como con lagunas el cuento de los tiempos, antes esmaltarlos con la luz y lustre de grandes cosas y hazañas, por sí mismos inventaron muchas hablillas y fábulas. ("Those who describe unknown regions of the world picture in their charts and maps, for the pleasure of those who look at them, scattered representations of fishes, beasts and birds, men in strange costumes, and grotesque faces and grimaces. They can do this with the more assurance since they know there is nobody who can accuse them of lying. The same thing has happened in the case of many historians, in my opinion, for where the light of history could not penetrate and ignorance of ancient things placed a kind of veil over their eyes, in order not to have to seek out such old, forgotten matters, they, in their solicitude to give glory to the people whose deeds they were describing—and to give greater amenity to their prose—and not to allow lacunae to appear in their account of past time, but rather to give their work brilliance by including great matters, invented a great number of fables out of their own heads"). Mézeray is cited by Hipp, p. 133.

41. Schulz, p. 120.

42. Ibid., p. 126.

43. Cirot, *Mariana historien,* p. 283.

44. Ibid., p. 294. Also, on the anti-Roman extravagances of Mariana's predecessors, including Ocampo, see Sverker Arnoldsson, *La leyenda negra. Estudios sobre sus orígenes* (Göteborg: Universitets Årsskrift, 1960), pp. 214–15.

45. This charitable reflection is that of Cirot, *Mariana historien*, p. 294.

46. Ibid., p. 297.

47. MS Egerton 1873, p. 70.

48. Cirot, *Mariana historien*, p. 48.

49. Hipp, p. 183.

50. On these incidents the best accounts are those of Thomas D. Kendrick, "An Example of the Theodicy-Motive in Antiquarian Thought," *Fritz Saxl 1890–1948. A Volume of Memorial Essays,* ed. D. J. Gordon (London: Nelson, 1957), pp. 309–25, and "False Chronicles", in *St. James in Spain* (London: Methuen, 1960), pp. 116–27. See also in this latter work "The Lead Books: 1595–1610", pp. 69–115. Kendrick identifies the authors as the Morisco archivists and translators Castillo and Luna, and also explains their apparent motives.

51. Cirot, *Mariana historien*, p. 45. Mariana gives his own etymology of the city's name "*Gar* in Arabic signifies cave, and a certain number of the soldiers who came over in the company of Tarif [*sic*] to conquer Spain, all of them natives of a city in Syria called Nata, set up their headquarters in that place. From *Gar* and *Nata* was made up the name of Granada, as prudent and erudite persons have supposed and stated. Others put forward different etymologies" (Book 25, Chapter 1). For the wide-ranging philological consequences of the controversy, see Werner Bahner, *La lingüística española del Siglo de Oro* (Madrid: Ciencia Nueva, 1966).

52. The decision to be sparing in the matter of reporting the marvelous may be inspired by a reading of Isidore also (cf. Bastett, p. 288).

53. On Pasquier and his disquisitions on Brunhilda, cf. Hay, p. 132.

54. Cirot, *Mariana historien*, p. 337.

55. On incipient skepticism even when religion is being touched upon, cf. Hay, p. 127, and on "common sense" as the new guiding notion, see Pasquier, p. 132. On a later Spanish scholar's concern, cf. Robert Jammes and Odette Gorsse, "Nicolás Antonio et le combat pour la vérité (31 lettres de Nicolás Antonio à Vázquez Siruela)" in *Hommage des Hispanistes français à Noël Salomon* (Barcelona: Laia, 1979), pp. 411–29. (Skepticism about Flavius Dexter in particular.)

56. "Respuesta," p. 60.

57. Cirot, *Mariana historien*, p. 170.

58. Reprinted in the Preface to Noguera's edition (Valencia: Monfort, 1783–96).

59. Cirot, *Mariana historien,* p. 176.

60. Apparently this word parodies *concinnator* ("unifier" or "harmonizer"), as used by, for instance, Salutati of historians (cf. Struever, p. 80). *Sarcinator* signifies a mere patcher of materials.

61. Cirot, *Mariana historien,* p. 178.

62. Ibid., pp. 181–84.

63. *General History,* Book 10, chapter 2.

64. Cirot, *Mariana historien,* p. 190.

65. Ibid., pp. 192–93, where the letter is reprinted.

66. Ibid., p. 195.

67. Ibid., pp. 207–209.

68. Gilimón de la Mota was also the judge appointed to try Mariana himself in 1610. Cirot, "Quelques lettres," pp. 20–22. On the documents surviving in the archives, see Ángel González Palencia, "Mantuano y Tamayo de Vargas," in *Del "Lazarillo" a Quevedo* (Madrid: C.S.I.C., 1946), pp. 207–29.

69. González Palencia, p. 214.

70. Ibid., pp. 217–18.

71. *Mantua* was a supposed Roman settlement on the site of Madrid, so that *madrileños* were, for the humanists, *mantuanos.*

72. González Palencia, p. 219.

73. Mantuano as a critic of historical writing is not negligible, and has had his defenders, e.g., Munárriz, and also A. Ludwig in his review of Cirot's book, *Archiv für das Studium der neueren Sprachen* 16 (1906):220–24.

74. The criticisms from this point onward are nugatory. A Captain Miguel Sanz de Venesa secured Mariana's alteration of the text in the matter of where the Franco-Spanish frontier runs: along the right or "French" bank of the Bidasoa, not midstream (1621).

75. Cirot, *Mariana historien,* p. 354.

76. Ibid., p. 348.

77. Gilbert, p. 387.

78. Cirot, *Mariana historien,* p. 343.

79. Ibid., p. 332.

80. The theory is that of J. G. A. Pocock, "The Origins of the Study of the Past," *Comparative Studies in Society and History* 4 (1962):243.

81. Hipp, p. 187, and Burke, p. 149, where he also notes a typical Jesuit position of disapproval of Tacitus, by Father Faminio Strada of the Roman College (1572–1649). Tacitus for him teaches readers of history to take in the plausible, not the actually true. He also uses the deplorable method of revealing secrets of state and of princes to the profane.

82. Burke studies this process in Tacitus's Spanish translator and emulator Álamos de Barrientos (1555–1643).

83. Cf. Hipp, p. 159, on the relation between the historians' and the early novelists' presentation of great persons. Figures such as Pedro the Cruel and Don Álvaro de Luna, who receive such patient coverage from Mariana, are favored protagonists of popular genres of literature: ballads and *comedias*.

84. Hipp, p. 138, citing Bussy-Rabutin (1622–66).

85. Hipp, p. 139, quotes Cardinal de Retz, who scorns *historiens vulgaires* as pretenders to knowing how to explain everything, whereas so many things in history are mysterious and will remain so.

86. See Hipp, p. 168, on the fascination these things hold for readers of history books. The innumerable volumes on the identity of the Man in the Iron Mask, or on the fate of the Dauphin in 1793, speak of a different attitude to history from Mariana's.

87. Cf. Pocock, "The Nature of Political Thought," *Colloquium*, No. 5 (1966):1–9, especially p. 8.

88. For Mariana (*On Death*, p. 140) even dreams and predictions are "echoes of providence".

89. The earlier uses of this adage, in the modern age usually attributed to George Santayana, are studied by Marie Schulz, p. 78. Gotfridus of Viterbo in his *History of the Popes* seems to inspire the words of John of Salisbury: *Aliena vita nobis magistra est, et qui ignarus est praeteritorum quasi secus in futurorum prorumpit eventus* ("The lives of others are our teachers, and whoever is ignorant of the past blunders into future events").

90. Pocock, "The Nature," p. 8.

91. Historical perspective is needed to assist in moralizing on past events, and perhaps it was for this reason that Mariana at first chose to stop his *History* at the year 1512.

92. Pocock, "The Origins," p. 243. Melchor Cano, writing around the year 1560, is an interesting figure in this respect: for him history is a subject distinct from rhetoric. History has its peculiar rules of evidence like those of law, and provides its own lessons, not necessarily similar to those taught by humanistic ethics. Cf. Hay, p. 129.

93. On Mariana and Vico, see Cirot, *Mariana historien*, p. 358.

Chapter Three

1. Such treatises are very numerous in the Middle Ages, and are often, under titles such as *Mirror of Princes* or *Secret of Secrets*, handy disguises for tracts on ordinary ethics, J. A. Fernández-Santamaría, *The State, War and*

Peace. Spanish Political Thought in the Renaissance, 1516–59 (New York: Cambridge University Press, 1977), discusses these, pp. 242–52.

2. Cf. *Isidori Hispalensis Episcopi Etymologiarum sive originum libri XX,* ed. W. M. Lindsay (Oxford: Oxford University Press, 1911), I.29.3 and IX.3.18. It is remarkable that Isidore illustrates the whole notion of "difference," fundamental to his method, by that between kings and tyrants, I.31.

3. Roland Mortier, *La Poétique des ruines en France* (Geneva: Droz, 1974), examines the place of ruins in the aesthetics of the age. In the view of medieval authors ruins were likely to be perceived as vestiges of the wrath of God (Mariana only invokes the continuing legend of the pagan Diana), or of irreversible loss (225). (Here we would be overingenious in equating Mariana's contemplation of the ruin with his coming consideration of the devastation of Castile's medieval institutions.) The sense of the immemorial (11), however, attaches itself poetically to Mariana's description; Nature is contemplated as the final sculptor of a former work of man (10), and Mariana shows how man, with groves and gardens, has embellished Nature's own work by imitating her. Incidentally, it would also be a hazardous thing to look for symbolic significance in the events of the "memorable autumn of 1599," with its floods, sickness, and plague of toads (and the death of the canon Juan Calderón), which, as Mariana says, accompanied the final stages of his writing *On the King.*

4. Cf. Guenter Lewy, *Constitutionalism and Statecraft During the Golden Age of Spain. A Study of the Political Philosophy of Juan de Mariana, S.J.* (Geneva: Droz, 1960). Lewy conveniently summarizes (39) the preceding writers who had apparently posited a Golden Age: Aeneas Sylvius (Enea Silvio Piccolomini, Pope Pius II, 1405–64), who situated it after the Fall, so that the corruption of man as a social being might not be a result of divine punishment; and Antonio de Guevara (1481–1545), who in his *Libro áureo de Marco Aurelio* (1529) asserted that the Golden Age lasted up to the time of Nimrod, the first tyrant.

5. Lewy, p. 47.

6. This is quite similar to the theory of Mariana's predecessor Fernando Vázquez de Menchaca (1512–69) in his *Controversiae illustres* (1559), who also derives politics from primitive human sociability, which in its turn is an aspect of Natural Law *(ius gentium naturale; ius gentium primaevum)* that has endowed man with right reason. It is only a divine dispensation in that Natural Law originates in Divine Providence. Vázquez, being a jurist, went on to posit the king as lawgiver and harmonizer of his laws with Nature's—a path that Mariana, of course, was temperamentally unprepared to follow. One may consult Peter Jochen Winters, *Die "Politik" des Johannes*

Althusius und ihre zeitgenössischen Quellen. Zur Grundlegung der politischen Wissenschaft im 16, und im beginnenden 17. Jahrhundert (Freiburg: Rombach, 1963), pp. 61–78, "Die spanischen Naturrechtslehrer [Vázquez and Diego de Covarrubias, 1512–77]"; pp. 84–86, "Mariana." Winters points out that Mariana, too, conceives of human sociability as *a mente divina hausta* ("emanated from the divine mind"), not as a product of necessity (84).

7. "God invented the rule of kings" is the phrase of Diego de Covarrubias: Lewy, p. 39. The divine invention of some form of government for men was a usual Jesuit position. Cf. Lewy, p. 41, on Luis de Molina and Francisco Suárez.

8. Cf. A. Duméril, "Un publiciste de l'Ordre des Jésuites calomnié: le Père Mariana," *Mémoires de l'Académie des Sciences, Inscriptions et Belles Lettres de Toulouse,* VIII Series, 7 (1885):83–146. Duméril points out the Isidorean origin (121) of this idea. The early Jesuit General Laínez had also proposed it.

9. Lewy, p. 60.

10. See Pierre Mesnard, *L'Essor de la philosophie politique au seizième siècle* (Paris: Vrin, 1952), pp. 549–66: "Mariana, ou le Déclin de l'humanisme." Mariana's apparently prudential ordering of his material is noted (558).

11. On Mariana and Erasmus, see Mesnard, p. 551. On Mariana and Machiavelli, see p. 562.

12. This was something of a humanistic commonplace. The French explorer of Brazil, Léry, noted it among his "noble savages" in the sixteenth century.

13. Cf. Fadrique Furió Ceriol, *El concejo y consejeros del príncipe* (Antwerp, 1559) ed. D. Sevilla Andrés; (Valencia: Diputación Provincial, 1952). On indiscriminate recruitment of civil servants, see p. 161. On *la fuerza y virtud de las señales del cuerpo* ("special value and excellences of certain physical characteristics," a topic Mariana does not discuss), pp. 151–57.

14. Mesnard, p. 565. The judicial assassination of Lanuza in 1591 already was an indication of the centralizing trend of the Spanish monarchy. The notorious traitor Antonio Pérez also made use of the Lanuza affair and the consequent ending of the special liberties of Aragon in his "monarchomach" writings: political aphorisms similar in tenor to Mariana's, but more acutely expressed.

15. On the state of the poor and of vagabonds at the time, see Michel Cavillac, "Introducción" to Cristóbal Pérez de Herrera, *Amparo de pobres* [1598]. (Madrid: Espasa, 1975), pp. 1–1ix and cvi–cxxix.

16. Cf. his remark in Chapter 11 of *On Death*: "An non vides cuncta in republica in gente perturbata et inversa, . . . inopum greges sine ope, sine lare familiari vagari, bella, famem, pestem, multis locis sine fine

grassari, quid dicam?" ("Can you not see over the whole state disorder and topsdyturvydom in the people, . . . flocks of indigents without resources, wandering without homes, in many places enduring warfare, hunger and disease, endlessly, what can I say?")

17. The celebrated phrase *se vive con libertad de conciencia* ("one lives with freedom of conscience"), said of Germany by the character Ricote in the *Second Part of Don Quijote* (1615), Chapter 54, is perhaps illuminated by this attitude on Mariana's part.

18. Cf. J. G. A. Pocock, pp. 1–9.

19. Mesnard, p. 552, points out the historical circumstances that attended the book's appearance. Loaisa authorized it in November 1598, but after the king's death, and during his own very short tenure of the Primatial See of Toledo. The royal privilege for publication came in January 1599, one month ahead of Loaisa's sudden death. Had the dying king examined the work personally, and had not the book been in the press, it might have been suppressed. The harsh words about the defeat of the Armada are:

Ne vicinae gentis calamitate et malis laetari possemus, paucis post annis numerosa clade amissa ad Angliae littora, eam plagam accepimus, eam ignominiam quam multi anni sanare non possint. Gravium scelerum quae in nostra gente vigent ea vindicta fuit, et nisi animus fallit, cuiusquam principis viri malae libidines divinum numen irritarunt; qui personae sacratae quam sustinebat oblitus, provectae atque adeo extremae aetatis immemor, intemperanter in licentiam se effudisse per idem tempus fama vulgabatur.

(Lest we should feel easy about rejoicing at the disasters afflicting a neighboring state, when a great loss was suffered on the coasts of England, we sustained that blow, that ignominy which many years will not be able to efface. That was the retribution exacted for grave delinquencies in our nation, and unless memory fails, it was the vile lusts of a certain prince which enraged the Divinity. This prince had forgotten the sacred personage he was, and the advanced age and even senility he had reached, and the rumor spread abroad that he had dissipated himself beyond reason in licentiousness.)

Cf. also, Lewy, p. 68. The source of the notion that pleasures can be the origin of the ruin of the state, however trivial they may seem, may be Cicero, *Of Old Age,* 12, 40. Cf. Hipp, p. 173.

20. See Robert Eccleshall, *Order and Reason in Politics. Theories of Absolute and Limited Monarchy in Early Modern England* (Oxford: Oxford University Press, 1978). He cites Justinian's *Institutes,* I.2.6, on the *lex regia* as the authority allowed by Roman law for the emperor being handed complete legislative power by the Roman people, p. 50. On the role of the medieval commercial classes in the progressive adoption of Roman law concepts, see Lewy, p. 59.

21. On the *Summa* of St. Thomas Aquinas as a political source-book, see Lewy, p. 15; Eccleshall, pp. 60–61. On a medieval lay authority for popular limitation of the king's powers, the *Defensor pacis* of Marsilio of Padua (1324), see Eccleshall, p. 64. To be fair, the Spanish juridical tradition is of comparable antiquity, that is, the *Siete partidas,* a comprehensive code established by King Alfonso X, the Wise.

22. This was the conception of political origins expounded, as we have seen, by the Spanish Natural-Law theorists Covarrubias and Vázquez de Menchaca (Winters, pp. 61–78). Also, on the sociability thesis, see Lewy, p. 44, who cites, as a clearer statement of Mariana's position, Book 19, Chapter 15 of his *General History.*

23. This episode occurs in the *General History,* Book 24, Chapter 16.

24. The same thought, expressed less stylishly, in the Preface to the Spanish version of the *General History:* "Ninguno se atreve a decir a los reyes la verdad; todos ponen la mira en sus particulares: miseria grande y que de ninguna cosa se padece mayor mengua en las casas reales. (No one dares tell kings the truth; everyone keeps his attention fixed on his own affairs: a great inconvenience and a thing that causes the greatest upsets in royal palaces).

25. Among the numerous writers and codifiers who passed this doctrine along to Renaissance political theorists was John of Salisbury. See Dorotea C. Macedo de Steffens, "La doctrina del tiranicidio. Juan de Salisbury (1115–80) y Juan de Mariana (1535–1625)," *Anales de historia antigua y medieval* 35 (1959):123–33. Also Bracton (before 1300), whose teaching that a ruler who refuses to bridle himself as he does others becomes a tyrant, is recalled by Eccleshall, p. 69, and Bartolo da Sassoferrato (1314–57), by Lewy, p. 57.

26. J. Roger Dunkle, "The Rhetorical Tyrant in Roman Historiography. Sallust, Livy and Tacitus," *Classical World* 65 (1971):12–20. The *libidines* and *scelera* which were laid at the door of the prince, and which could be invoked as provocations to divine retribution in destroying the Armada, were probably commonplaces from Roman historians. The aging Philip II would consequently be innocent of them in fact, cf. note 19 above.

27. Lewy, p. 133.

28. Ibid., p. 135.

29. Ibid., pp. 136–37. This fear on the part of monarchs is described by Pierre Bayle, *Dictionaire historique et critique,* 4th ed. (Amsterdam and Leiden: P. Brunel, 1730), 3:329.

30. For the term monarchomach, see Lewy, p. 16. On secularization and its consequences for theories of resistance, see Enrique Tierno Galván, "Introducción", *Antología de escritores políticos del Siglo de Oro,* ed. P. de Vega (Madrid: Taurus, 1966), p. 3–14.

31. Furió Ceriol, p. 108, cf. note 13 above.

32. Lewy, pp. 48–49.

33. On the thoughtlessness of Mariana on this subject, see Lewy, pp. 100–1, and on more enlightened opinions in other places, J. R. Hale, "Sixteenth Century Explanations of War and Violence," *Past and Present,* No. 51 (1971):3–26.

34. The term is Duméril's, p. 114.

35. Diego de Saavedra Fajardo, *Corona gótica* (Münster: J. Janson, 1646), I:9. This is the work of a theorist of absolutism who had witnessed the disasters of the Thirty Years' War.

36. *General History,* Book 15, Chapter 4.

37. Lewy, pp. 67, 91.

38. Mesnard, pp. 562, 566.

39. Lewy, pp. 107–10.

40. Pedro Urbano González de la Calle calls him a "sentimental collectivist" in his "Ideas político-morales del Padre Juan de Mariana," *Revista de archivos, bibliotecas y museos,* 31 (1914):201–28.

41. Much of Chapter 9 of Book 3 is taken up by a laudatory description of the Escorial. The nerveless state of Spain in his own times, brought on by the slackening of this cohesion, is portrayed in *On Death* (359–60):

Quod aetatis vitium est tamen, gentis mores longa oratione accusavimus. Homines ad arma natos affluenti copia voluptatum, illecebris, omnis amoenitatis maritimae terrestrisque atque commercio gentium externarum ad famam accurrenti nostrarum copiarum, easque importantium merces quibus corpora debilitantur, vigor animorum extinguitur, enervari et peregrinis moribus depravari; atque ita ut nec libidini nec sumptibus, nec vestium pretio modum faciant, accubantes in conviviis, cibo atque vino debilitatos, emollitos atque corruptos stupris exemplo principum lascivire populares. Quidquid alibi per partes corruptum est, quasi confusis omnium gentium vitiis in mores Hispanorum migrasse. Unde quasi ex summo praecipitante fortuna graves calamitates imminere ac vero iam instare videantur.

("That, however, is the vice of the age, and we have found fault with the morality of our nation at great length. Men born to arms are rendered nerveless and are depraved by strange habits, by the search for pleasures, by yielding to allurements, by their contacts with foreign peoples who flock to the news of our prosperity, and by the importation of those very products by which bodies are enfeebled and the powers of the mind are dulled. In the same way, the common people also behave wantonly, setting no limits to sensual pleasure, to the money they spend, or to the price of their apparel. They recline at their banquets, besotted with food and wine, softened and corrupted by debauchery, after the example of their princes [this phrase was struck out, of course, by Mariana's censors]. Almost everywhere a decay is setting in, as though by contagion from the vices of all nations it had seeped into the morality of Spain. For this reason, now that Fortune is toppling down from her peak, fearsome calamities are in the offing, nay they are truly now upon us").

42. On Mariana's ideas as a halfway stage to the theory of *Ratio status (Razón de estado)*, see Lewy, p. 111. The Neo-Stoic Lipsius, working in the Spanish Netherlands, had already theorized that the well-being of the state should be allowed to repose on and spring from the *sapientia* of the ruler alone. Also, see Pocock, p. 5, for the inconveniences occasioned by constitution-making. To make a constitution would be at that time an innovative step, and an admission that political stability did not exist; otherwise the ancient body of constitutional law would have sufficed.

43. Bayle, p. 330.

44. These included Bodin, Du Plessis-Mornay, and La Noue. All were combated, however, by Mariana's friend and fellow-member of the Society, Pedro de Rivadeneira in his *Tratado de la religión y virtudes que debe tener el príncipe cristiano* (Madrid: P. Madrigal, 1595), and this illustrates the paradox that the political theorists of the Society of Jesus should also be "monarchomachs": see Lewy, p. 137. The treatise of the much earlier French theorist Claude de Seyssel, written to coincide with the accession of the first Valois king François I, was read by the monarchomachs, bears many similarities to Mariana's work in its composition and chief principles, and has the unusual distinction of being still read, according to J. H. Hexter, "Claude de Seyssel and Normal Politics in the Age of Machiavelli," *Art, Science and History in the Renaissance,* ed. Charles Singleton (Baltimore: Johns Hopkins University Press, 1967), pp. 389–415. Seyssel's *La Mon-*

archie de France infers its principles from a study of the previous three or four reigns in France alone, and is similarly concerned to regulate the new royal power in the spirit of ancient law. Religion, justice, and the police are the necessary "bridles" restraining the potential tyrant, not legislative assemblies. An early English monarchomach, in opposition to Queen Mary I, was John Ponet, in his *Short Treatise of Politique Power* (n.p. [Strasbourg?], 1556).

45. Lewy, p. 138.

46. Recent works on the assassination are those of Philippe Erlanger, *L'Étrange Mort de Henri IV* (Paris: Perrin, 1972), and Roland Mousnier, *L'Assassinat d'Henri IV* (Paris: Gallimard, 1964).

47. The *Anti-Mariana* of Roussel (1611) was the chief of these, cf. Bayle, p. 330.

48. Lewy, p. 143.

49. Ibid., p. 144.

50. Also perhaps because of their dislike of the way Mariana's German Protestant publisher, Wichel, had overprinted the work's 1611 edition to damage Jesuit reputations and spread abroad references to the vices of Catholic princes, cf. Bayle, p. 330, citing Coton.

51. Lewy, p. 161.

52. Ibid., p. 59.

53. Bagehot's five points in favor of the monarchy of, e.g., Queen Victoria, are (1) it is intelligible, while it preserves the mystique of heroic ages; (2) it is a religious strengthening for the secularized state; (3) the monarch assumes the social headship, and is at the center of all that is best; (4) the monarch assumes the moral headship; (5) the real organs of power can be allowed to evolve out of sight. Cf. *Walter Bagehot. A Study . . . Together with a Selection from His Political Writings,* ed. N. St. John-Stevas (Bloomington: Indiana University Press, 1959), "The Monarchy," pp. 247–80.

Chapter Four

1. Cicero's piece probably in its turn imitated the lost *De luctu* [On Mourning] of Crantor, a work many Classical authors cite as though definitive of the genre. The topics, moral and historical, such a *consolatio* might contain are all similar to those chosen by Mariana (in the strictly consolatory portions of his work). In his *Tusculanae disputationes* (III), Cicero sketches such a work; among his successors in the genre are Seneca, St. Ambrose *(De fide resurrectionis),* St. Jerome *(Letter 55, to Heliodorus),* and Enrique de Villena *(Tratado de la consolación).* Derek C. Carr, in his "In-

troducción" (lxxiv–xcvi) to his edition of this last work (Madrid: Espasa-Calpe, 1976), shows how Villena's treatise is also a progression from *sententia* to *sententia* rather than a logical discourse, and also betrays a rather unfeeling attitude toward the man consoled, Juan Fernández de Valera, who had lost all his relatives in a plague.

2. These innovations in the Renaissance dialogue are studied by Antonio Castro Díaz, *Los* Coloquios *de Pedro Mexía* (Sevilla: Diputación Provincial, 1977), 36–37. See also Pierre Boyancé, *Études sur l'humanisme cicéronien* (Brussels: Latomus, 1970), for many of Mariana's models.

3. Indeed rather a "jest in earnest," retelling the anecdote first included by Seneca in his *Moral Epistles:* Pacuvius, Prefect of Syria, followed the custom of offering himself funeral feasts every night of his life, after which his attendants would carry him off to bed chanting, "His life is ended! His life is ended!" as though it were the truth. A more correct text is in Pauly, Wissowa, Kroll, eds. *Real-Encyklopädie der klassischen Altertumswissenschaft* Stuttgart: Metzler, 1894–, *s.v.* "Pacuvius [3]," vol. 36, col. 2158.

4. Mariana draws up an analogy with all laws that hold heirs of a malefactor to be liable. So, sin may have been purged, but a *reatum* or stigma remains for the heirs of Adam to bear.

5. Michael J. Woods, *The Poet and the Natural World in the Age of Góngora* (Oxford: Oxford University Press, 1978), pp. 11–12.

6. Ibid., p. 83–84. An excellent account of this topic is to be found in Jeffrey B. Spencer, *Heroic Nature Ideal Landscape in English Poetry from Marvell to Thomson* (Evanston, Ill.: Northwestern University Press, 1973), "Before 1650," pp. 3–49.

7. Woods, p. 8.

8. These games do not appear, probably because there is no clear Classical precedent for them, in the *Días geniales o lúdricos* of Rodrigo Caro (1573–1647), friend of many Jesuits. The recent edition is by Jean-Pierre Étienvre (Madrid: Espasa, 1978).

9. The visit of St. James to Spain achieved its place in the Breviary in 1625, after action by Pope Urban VIII. On the whole controversy, see Kendrick, *St. James in Spain.*

10. In his notes for a letter to the king [Egerton MS 1873] Mariana complains: "El día de hoy reina en España un deseo extraordinario de hallar y aun, con ligera ocasión, forjar nuevos nombres de reliquias de santos ("At the present time there overwhelms the land of Spain an inordinate desire to discover and even on flimsy evidence to counterfeit new names for saints' relics." December 20, 1597).

11. Cirot, *Mariana historien,* pp. 80–84.

12. Cf. Manuel Díaz y Díaz, "Jacobus-Legende bei Isidorus," *Historisches Jahrbuch* 77 (1958):467–71.

13. Díaz y Díaz, "Antigua literatura relacionada con Santiago el Mayor," *Compostellanum* 11 (1966):664–66.

14. Mariana himself uses the phrase.

15. On this clerical enmity to theaters, cf. the recent work of Antonio García Berrio, *Intolerancia de poder y protesta popular en el Siglo de Oro. Los debates sobre la licitud moral del teatro* (Málaga: Universidad de Málaga, 1978). On the earlier, Patristic period of the debate, see p. 24.

16. Ibid., p. 20.

17. The older and still uniquely authoritative study and anthology of clerical judgments in the debate is that of Emilio Cotarelo y Mori, *Bibliografía de las controversias sobre la licitud del teatro en España. . . . Dictámenes de jurisconsultos, moralistas y teólogos . . .* (Madrid: Revista de Archivos, Bibliotecas y Museos, 1904), "Juan de Mariana," pp. 430ff., on Camos, p. 18.

18. García Berrio, p. 24.

19. Ibid., p. 26. A powerful defense of the theater from the point of view of its beneficent potentialities was, in those very years, that of Alonso López, el Pinciano, *Philosophía antigua poética* [1596], ed. A. Carballo Picazo (Madrid: C.S.I.C., 1953), III:17–18, 263–65.

20. García Berrio, p. 30. Even in 1630, however, a Jesuit, Pedro Puente Hurtado de Mendoza, revived the venomous attack in his *De fide*, concentrating once again on offstage behavior. Cotarelo, p. 22.

21. García Berrio, p. 30.

22. Mariana's notes taken from Aelius Aristides cover pp. 99–121 of Egerton MS 1871. The life of Aelius Aristides is in C. A. Behr, *Aelius Aristides and the Sacred Tales* (Amsterdam: Hakkert, 1968). We read of the following relevant orations: *Against the Dancers,* deploring erotic miming, p. 88 and n. 91b; *On the Prohibition of Comedy* (c. A.D. 157–165), deploring "jests from wagons" and their corrupting effects on children, pp. 95–96 and n. 5; *Against Those Who Mock the Mysteries* (A.D. 170), deploring singsong delivery and gesticulations imitated from whores, p. 107.

23. Cotarelo, p. 9.

24. Ibid., p. 430.

25. Mariana's apparent interest in Pythagorean speculations has been noticed before, in his lecture (391) to the diffident Decanus of *On Death and Immortality.*

26. García Berrio, p. 34.

27. The two sets of regulations *(Ordenanzas),* for Seville and Toledo, are listed as documents 25 and 26 of the volume Egerton MS 1873, ff.

155–57b, but they have been removed. Also gone is a copy of *Las coplas del Tabefe,* the nature of which is unknown.

28. Mariana is fond of this demonstration, that in the midst of life we are in death; it occurs also in *On Death,* p. 364. He also rejects the argument that bullfighting provides an incentive to the industry of breeding horses. Breeding better horses only to destroy them in the bullring is an absurdity, and this implacable hater of the whole ethos of the *caballero* suggests that mule-breeding, which benefits the common man, ought to supplant it.

29. Cotarelo, p. 36.

30. García Berrio, p. 64.

31. Ibid., p. 37.

32. Stuart Clark, "Witchcraft and Kingship," *apud* Sydney Anglo, ed., *The Damned Art* (London: Routledge, 1977), pp. 156–81.

33. Gellio appears in no catalogue of printed works.

34. The ancient weights and measures are set against the Spanish, and specifically the Toledan ones of Mariana's day.

35. E. Mary Smallwood, *The Jews Under Roman Rule.* (Leiden: Brill, 1977), p. 168, n. 82. The date "5,228 years from the beginning of the world" given by Isidore would not be doubted by Mariana. Cf. Paul Merritt Bastett, "The Use of History in the *Chronicon* of Isidore of Seville," *History and Theory* 15 (1976):287.

Chapter Five

1. Mir, 2:672.

2. The comparison between the prose-rhythm of Mariana's Latin (and possibly even his Spanish) and that of his model Livy should perhaps be undertaken by a Latinist; cf. Hans Aili, *The Prose Rhythm of Sallust and Livy* (Stockholm: University of Stockholm, 1979).

3. Cirot, *Mariana historien,* p. 365.

4. Ibid., p. 376. Usually at the beginnings of books of the *History* (Bk. 20; Bk. 21) or, for example, in passages of heightened description like that of the city of Granada (Book 16, chapter 16).

5. Munárriz, 2:160–61. This author is displeased, however, by other features, such as Mariana's identical turns of phrase to be used when he really has nothing to say (on the state of Spain at the death of Sancho el Mayor of Navarre, or at the death of Alfonso XI of Castile), 3:256.

6. Cirot studies an entire area of these archaisms, the conjugated forms of verbs, in his article "Quelques remarques sur les archaïsmes de Mariana et la langue des prosateurs de son temps," *Romanische Forschungen* 23 (1907):883–904. The study is comparative, with citations from some thirty

contemporary authors. The forms Cirot examines are the past subjunctive second-person plural in -*áredes* / -*éredes*, the preterite indicative second-person plural in -*stes;* the alternative future and conditional forms such as *pornía, ternía,* and *vernía* and those derived from compounds of these; the form *habemos; ovo, oviera, oviese,* etc.; conjugated forms of the verb to see: *vía, ver,* etc.; the pluperfect indicative in -*ara* / -*iera;* and the use of *ser* as auxiliary verb in compound tenses. Forms identical with modern usage are noted, and ascribed tentatively to assistants in translation or to printers.

7. José Godoy Alcántara, cited by Benito Sánchez Alonso, 2:172. Godoy wrote, of course (1868) at a moment when the destined Bourbon successor to the throne, as Alfonso XII, was an adolescent himself.

8. The fullest account of the phenomenon of Renaissance Latin poetry and of the Society's cultivation of the art is that of Edmond Pognon, *Encyclopédie de la Pléiade. Histoire des littératures. II* (Paris: Gallimard, 1956), pp. 291–307. John Addington Symonds, in *The Renaissance in Italy. The Revival of Learning* (New York: Holt, 1881), p. 473, points out how Girolamo Vida had, in the early sixteenth century, recommended the teaching of bucolic verse composition as an exercise. He also notes Vida's insistence, in his *Ars poetica,* on the aspiring poet's profit from physical exercise and games. Though Mariana never attempts verse in the vernacular, he seems not to despise it, since in the *General History* he speaks well of the work of Petrarch (Book 16, chapter 13) and of that of Ausiàs March (Book 23, chapter 3).

9. The situation in our own age for the appreciation of Renaissance Latin poetry is studied by Francesco Tateo, "La poesia latina del Rinascimento," *Cultura e scuola* 3, No. 10 (1964):13–21.

10. The technique of assembling "poetical memories" is described by Giuseppe Velli, "La memoria poetica del Petrarca," *Italia medioevale e umanistica* 19 (1976):172–207. On new settings, see p. 204. Also Tateo, p. 14.

11. On "atmosphere," see Velli, pp. 204, 206.

12. On the comparison with landscape-painting, see Leo Spitzer, "The Problem of Latin Renaissance Poetry," in *Romanische Literaturstudien* (Tübingen: Niemeyer, 1959), pp. 923–44.

13. Velli, p. 186.

14. Woods, p. 2. Also Spencer, p. 16, distinguishes between "inspirational" and "recreational" landscapes.

15. Woods, p. 49.

16. Spencer, p. 23, discusses the "decorative" type among his heroic landscapes, and its prototype in the garden of Alcinous's palace in Homer's

Odyssey VII. The emphasis falls upon the dexterity of the workers in the garden, on the fruits and their seasons, and on the two irrigating streams.

17. Symonds, pp. 498–501, describes the works of the most talented of these poets of rusticity in Renaissance Italy, Marcantonio Flaminio of Imola. This poet has also a poem on a country excursion with two friends, for study and comment on the Classics; this resembles the design of *On Death and Immortality.*

18. Cirot, "Une élégie latine du P. Mariana avec la réponse," *Mélanges de littérature, d'histoire et de philologie offerts à Paul Laumonier* (Paris: Droz, 1935), pp. 369–76, gives the text (Egerton 1875, here more accurately copied) and also the reply in verse of a more prosaic cast by Castellón, pp. 375–76. He identifies Villaminaya, a place near Orgaz, as inhabited at least until 1850, p. 370.

19. Symonds, p. 464, indicates that the Italian Poliziano had in his day also written an elegy on the death of a friend's wife.

20. Pedro Urbano González de la Calle, "Ideas político-morales del P. Juan de Mariana," *Revista de Archivos, Bibliotecas y Museos* 32 (1915):409–10.

21. Cirot, "Une élégie," p. 373, n. 4.

22. Robin Carter, "*Fuenteovejuna* and Tyranny. Some Problems of Linking Drama with Political Theory," *Forum for Modern Language Studies* 13 (1977):313–25.

23. Otis H. Green, "La dignidad real en la literatura del Siglo de Oro. Notículas de un estudioso," *Revista de filología española* 48 (1965):231–50. A recent work of reconstruction of the past, Francisco Ayala's *El doliente,* is related to its origins in Mariana by Gonzalo Sobejano, "Lectura de *El doliente,*" *Cuadernos hispanoamericanos,* Nos. 329–30 (1977):449–68.

24. Lewy, p. 156.

25. Cited by Leo F. Solt, *Saints in Arms* (Stanford: Stanford University Press, 1959), pp. 86–88.

26. The application of principles resembling Mariana's at an inopportune time in Poland in the second half of the eighteenth century effectively ensured the partition and destruction of the kingdom.

27. José Cepeda Adán, "Una visión de América a fines del siglo XVI: las Indias en la *Historia* del P. Mariana," *Estudios americanos* 6 (1953):397–421.

28. In general Munárriz thinks Mariana's style is "majestic," 2:154. Details he finds worthy of censure are a tendency to place adverbs where an orator would place them, and this does not carry over into written prose (1:337); overuse of parentheses (1:288), and here might be classified many of Mariana's sentences without verbs, noticed above; there is no significant difference in their effect on the flow of the prose; mixing of metaphorical and plain styles (Munárriz cites the point in the *General History* where the

young Henry III of Castile "drops the pilot," in this case the Archbishop of Santiago. In his rueful speech the Archbishop likens the king's minority to a navigation, but then moves to abstracts like "prudence" and "benignity," rather than continuing the sea-metaphor, II, 54). Cirot, *Mariana historien,* p. 376, gives some reasons why this style does not date: it is not ostentatious, avoiding condensation, antitheses, figurative pretentiousness or easy irony. On the other hand some other age may not care for his Ciceronian redundancy of verbs, adjectives in pairs, and the like.

29. A typical work was his anthology *Juan de Mariana, cantor de España. Selección y estudio* (Madrid: Fe, 1943).

30. Enrique Tierno Galván.

31. Bayle, p. 333.

32. Cirot, "Le roman du P. Mariana," *Bulletin hispanique* 22 (1920): 269–94.

Chapter Six

1. Perhaps Mariana is one of the first authors to give the city of Paris its celebrated name of *La Ville-Lumière (lux orbis terrarum).*

2. Enrique Tierno Galván speculates on the social pressures to produce a book that may underlie a large number of publications by clerical writers, all unoriginal and repetitive, in a middle region between moral philosophy and political projecting.

3. For the "utopian," "artificially traditional" aspects of the past, which were thought to be important for posterity by historians, cf. Pocock, p. 209. For the actual, sanguine view of Spain and its probable future held by those who were not historians, cf. J. H. Elliott. "Self-Perception and Decline in Early Seventeenth Century Spain," *Past and Present,* No. 74 (1977):41–61.

4. On the innovation that theories of absolutism represented, cf. Robert Ashton, *The English Civil War* (London: Weidenfeld, 1978), pp. 12–21, 42.

Selected Bibliography

PRIMARY SOURCES

Historiae de rebus Hispaniae libri XX. Toledo: Petrus Roderici, 1592.

Historiae de rebus Hispaniae. Libri XXV. Toledo: Pedro Rodríguez, 1592; reprinted Toledo: Tomás Guzmán, 1595, and in the collection *Hispaniae illustratae.* Edited by Andreas Schottius. Frankfurt: C. Marnius and the Heirs of Aubrius, 1603–8.

De ponderibus et mensuris. Toledo: Tomás Guzmán, 1599; reprinted Mainz: Balthasar Lipp, 1605.

De rege et regis institutione. Libri III. Toledo: Pedro Rodríguez, 1599; reprinted Mainz: Balthasar Lipp, 1605 and 1609.

Historia general de España. Compuesta primero en latín, buelta al castellano. Toledo: Pedro Rodríguez, 1601; reprinted Madrid: Luis Sánchez, 1608, and Viuda de Alonso Martín (Volume I) and Juan de la Cuesta (Volume II), 1617–18.

Historiae de rebus Hispaniae. Libri XXX. Mainz: A. Weichelius, 1605.

Tractatus VII. De adventu B. Iacobi Apostoli in Hispaniam. Pro editione vulgata. De spectaculis. De monetae mutatione. De die mortis Christi. De annis Arabum. De morte et immortalitate. Cologne: Antonius Hieratus, 1609.

Scholia in Vetus et Novum Testamentum. Madrid: Luis Sánchez, 1619.

Summarium ad Historiam Hispaniae eorum quae acciderunt annis sequentibus. Mainz: Daniel and David Aubry, and Clement Schleich, 1619.

Historia general de España. Compuesta, emendada y añadida por el Dr. J. de M. Madrid: Luis Sánchez (Volume I) and Toledo: Pedro Rodríguez (Volume II), 1623; reprinted Madrid: Francisco Martínez, 1635; Madrid: Carlos Sánchez, 1650; Madrid: Andrés García de la Iglesia, n.d. [c. 1670]; Madrid: Jerónimo Rojo, 1733–41; Antwerp [really Lyon]: Publisher unnamed, 1733–39 and 1751–56; Madrid: Joaquín Ibarra, 1780; Valencia: Monfort, 1783–96.

Discurso de las enfermedades de la Compañia de Jesús. Madrid: Gabriel Ramírez, 1768. (A second Spanish presentation of the text of this work is that of E. Barriobero y Herrán. Madrid: Mundo Latino, 1931).

" 'Respuesta' [to a letter of Bartolomé Leonardo de Argensola, 1602] *apud*
   Juan Antonio Pellicer y Saforcada." In *Ensayo de una biblioteca de
   traductores españoles*. Madrid: Antonio de Sancha, 1778, pp. 59–62.
"Epitafio del Padre Pedro de Rivadeneira, S.J." [1611] *apud* José Eusebio
   Nieremberg, S.J. *Vidas ejemplares de algunos varones ilustres de la
   Compañía*. Madrid: Alonso de Paredes, 1647. Volume 4, p. 447.
"Escritos sueltos" [some routine *pareceres* of Mariana's on ecclesiastical pro-
   cedure]. *Obras. Colección dispuesta y revisada por F[rancisco] P[i] y
   M[argall]*. Madrid: Rivadeneyra, 1854 ("Biblioteca de Autores Es-
   pañoles," 30–31). Volume 2, pp. 619–25.
"Elegy" [consoling his friend Castejón, or Castellón, on the deaths of his
   wife and infant daughter]. Edited (with some incorrections) from
   British Library Ms Egerton 1875 by Georges Cirot. "Une élégie latine
   du P. Mariana avec la réponse." *Mélanges de Littérature, d'histoire et de
   philologie offerts à Paul Laumonier*. Paris: Droz, 1935, pp. 374–75.

SECONDARY SOURCES

1. Continuations of Mariana's *General History*
Miñana, José Manuel. *Historiae de rebus Hispaniae libri XXX. Accedunt Fr.
   Iosephi Emmanuelis Minianae . . . continuationis novae libri X*. The
   Hague: Petrus de Hond, 1633. Later translated into Spanish by Vi-
   cente Romero. Madrid: Benito Cano, 1794–95.
Espinosa y Malo, Félix Lucio de. *Historia general de España. Ahora nuevamente
   añadido por F. L. de E. y M.* Madrid: Andrés García de la Iglesia,
   1678; reprinted Lyon: Briasson, 1719, Madrid: Joaquín Ibarra, 1780,
   and Andrés Ramírez, 1780–82.
Sabán y Blanco, José. *Historia general de España. Enmendada, añadida e
   ilustrada, con notas históricas y críticas . . . hasta la muerte de Carlos III*.
   Madrid: Núñez de Vargas, 1817–21; reprinted Valencia: López,
   1830–41.
Toreno, Conde de. *Historia general de España . . . hasta el año de 1808.
   Aumentada con todos los sucesos que comprenden la historia de su levanta-
   miento, guerra y revolución, escrita por el C. de T. . . . hasta el pronun-
   ciamiento de 1 de septiembre de 1840*. Madrid: González, 1841–43.
Toreno, Conde de, and Chao, Eduardo. [Same title as above.] Madrid:
   Gaspar y Roig, 1848–51; reprinted with slight changes by the same
   authors, 1852–53.

2. Translations into Spanish

Anon. *Del rey y de la institución de la dignidad real. Traducido de la segunda edición (1640)*. Madrid: Sociedad Literaria y Tipográfica, 1845.

Pi y Margall, Francisco. "Sobre los juegos públicos" and "Sobre la alteración de la moneda." In his edition cited above ("Biblioteca de Autores Españoles") of 1854, II. Revisions and modernizations of translations by Mariana himself. A translation of *De rege* by an unknown hand is in the same edition.

3. Translations into English

Laures, John. *The Political Economy of Juan de Mariana*. With a Foreword by Edwin R. A. Seligman. New York: Fordham University Press, 1928.

Moore, George A. *The King and the Education of the King*. Translated from the Latin First Edition. Washington, D.C.: Country Dollar Press, 1948.

Stevens, John (Captain). *The General History of Spain, from the First Peopling of it by Tubal till the Death of King Ferdinand, . . . with a Continuation to the Death of King Philip III. With Two Supplements, by Friar Ferdinand de Salcedo [and] . . . Friar Basil Varén de Soto*. London: R. Sare, F. Saunders and T. Bennett, 1699.

4. Books and Articles about Mariana and His Works

Asensio, Félix, S.J. "El profesorado de Juan de Mariana y su influjo en la vida del escritor." *Hispania* [Madrid] 13 (1953):581–639.

Cepeda Adán, José. "Una visión de América a fines del siglo XVI: las Indias en la *Historia* del P. Mariana." *Estudios americanos* 6 (1953):397–421.

Cirot, Georges. *Études sur l'Historiographie espagnole: Mariana historien*. Bordeaux: Féret, 1905. The primary work on the author, judicious and never superseded.

———. "La famille de Juan de Mariana." *Bulletin hispanique* 6 (1904):309–31.

———. "Mariana jésuite: la jeunesse." *Bulletin hispanique* 38 (1936):295–352. Corrects and augments what Cirot had stated about Mariana's early career in his book, *supra*.

———. "Les portraits du P. Juan de Mariana." *Bulletin hispanique* 7 (1905):409–11.

———. "À propos du 'De rege,' des *Septem tractatus* de Mariana et de son ou de ses procès." *Bulletin hispanique* 10 (1908):95–99.

———. "Quelques lettres de Mariana et nouveaux documents sur son procès." *Bulletin hispanique* 19 (1917):1–25.

————. "Quelques remarques sur les archaïsmes de Mariana et la langue des prosateurs de son temps: Conjugaison." *Romanische Forschungen* 23 (1907):883–904.

————. "Le roman du P. Mariana." *Bulletin hispanique* 22 (1920):269–94. On the German Romantic novel, attributed here to Friedrich Buchholz.

Duméril, A. "Un publiciste de l'Ordre des Jésuites calomnié: le Père Mariana." *Mémoires de l'Académie des Sciences, Inscriptions et Belles Lettres de Toulouse,* Series VIII, 7 (1885):83–146. Enthusiastic plea for the author as a political genius, and a kind of culture-hero in many realms of human endeavor.

García Villada, Z. "El P. Juan de Mariana, historiador." *Razón y Fe* 69 (1924):455–62. On Mariana's critical method and his providentialist, patriotic outlook.

Garzón, Francisco de Paula, S.J. *El Padre Juan de Mariana y las escuelas liberales: Estudio comparativo.* Madrid: Ciencia Cristiana, 1889. Only worth mentioning as an early rejoinder to the enthusiastic adoption of Mariana as a precursor by Liberal publicists such as Pi y Margall.

González de la Calle, Pedro Urbano. "Algunas notas complementarias acerca de las ideas morales del Padre Juan de Mariana." *Revista de Archivos, Bibliotecas y Museos* 39 (1918):267–87; and 40 (1919):130–40; 231–47; 418–30, 536–51. Continuing González de la Calle's judicious reading of *On Public Shows* and, for the first time in detail anywhere, of *On Death and Immortality.*

————. "Ideas político-morales del P. Juan de Mariana." *Revista de Archivos, Bibliotecas y Museos* 29 (1913):388–406; 30 (1914):46–60, 201–28; 31 (1914):242–62; and 32 (1915):400–19. Sympathetically written survey of the ideas in *On the King* and *On Alterations in the Value of Currency.*

González Palencia, Ángel. "Mantuano y Tamayo de Vargas" [1924] in *Del "Lazarillo" a Quevedo.* Madrid: C.S.I.C., pp. 207–29.

Lewy, Guenter. *Constitutionalism and Statecraft during the Golden Age of Spain. A Study of the Political Philosophy of Juan de Mariana, S.J.* Geneva: Droz, 1960 ("Travaux d'Humanisme et Renaissance," 36). The only book entirely on Mariana and his political thought in English. Sympathetic to his positions, and arguing cogently in respect of what Mariana did not stand for, in spite of the assumptions of many writers. A rich bibliography.

Macedo de Steffens, Dorotea. "La doctrina del tiranicidio: Juan de Salisbury (1115–80) y Juan de Mariana (1535–1624)." *Anales de historia antigua y medieval,* 35 (1959): 123–33. Illustrates how traditional Mariana really is in his views.

Mesnard, Pierre. "Mariana ou le déclin de l'humanisme." *L'Essor de la philosophie politique au XVIe siècle.* Paris: Vrin, 1952, pp. 549–66. Contains a clear synopsis of *On the King,* and sets that work in its sixteenth-century context.

Norris, Frank I. "Mariana and the Classical Tradition of Statecraft." *Kentucky Romance Quarterly* 24 (1977):389–97. Explores, among other topics, the possible influence of Mariana on Thomas Jefferson.

Index

absolutism, 66, 91, 110, 126n35
Acevedo, Francisco de, Archbishop
   of Burgos, 18
Acosta, José de, 12
Acquaviva, Claudio, 5th. General
   of the Jesuits, 68
actors, 85, 87, 88, 130n20
Aelius Aristides, 87, 88, 90,
   130n22
agriculture, 65–66, 79
Alcalá, University of, 4, 85
Alcocer, Fray Francisco de, 85
Alemán, Mateo, 96
Aliaga, Luis de, 13, 17, 18
Alonso de Herrera, Gabriel, 2
Annius of Viterbo, 34
aphorisms, 19, 105, 106, 111,
   123n14
Aragon, liberties of, 28, 123n14
arbitristas, 18, 30, 110
archaisms, 97, 106, 131–32n6
Armada, Invincible, 15, 56, 85,
   124n19, 125n26
asceticism, 76–78
assemblies, 52, 53, 55, 56, 58,
   59, 93, 110
astrology, 1, 37
Augustine, St., 81
Augustinian Order, 11, 85, 86

Bagehot, Walter, 69, 128n53
Ballesteros, Manuel, 106
Baronius, Cardinal (Cesare
   Baronio), 82, 83
Barrière, Jean de La, 67
Bayle, Pierre, 20, 60, 106
beekeeping, 2, 92
Belilla, bell of, 38
Bellarmine, St. Robert, 60, 68,
   76, 93
Berengaria (Berenguela), Queen of
   Castile and León, 3, 42
Beza, Théodore de Bèze, called
   Theodorus, 6
bishops, 50, 53, 54, 58, 95, 110,
   114n39
Blanche (Blanca), Queen of
   France, 3, 42
Boccaccio, Giovanni, 36
Bolingbroke, Henry St. John,
   Viscount, 69
brothels, 89, 90–91, 111
Brunhilda (Brunehaut), Queen of
   the Franks, 36
Buchholz, Friedrich, 107
bullfighting, 3–4, 91, 111,
   131n28

Calderón, Juan, Canon of Toledo,
   48, 122n3

calendars, 92, 93
Camos, Fray Marco Antonio de, 86
Cano, Fray Melchor, 121n92
Carlos, Don, 49, 73, 77, 94
Carmena, 71, 73, 74
Carvallo, Luis Alfonso de, 87
Castellionius (Castellón or Castejón), 104
Castilian language, 2, 96–97, 98
Castro, Guillén de, 104, 105
Catalina, Duchess of Savoy, 86
Catalina de Santa Ana, Sor, 2, 3, 14, 15
Cava, la, 29, 44
censorship, 10, 84, 87
Cervantes, Miguel de, 87, 96, 106; *Don Quijote de la Mancha,* 41, 48, 88, 97, 124n17
Charles V, Holy Roman Emperor (Charles I of Spain), 18, 30, 31, 52, 84, 97, 113n23
Charles VII, King of France, 94
Chastel, Jean, 67, 68
chemistry, 72, 78, 92
China, 95
chronicles, 25, 45, 93, 97–98, 117n18
chronology, 92–93
Cicero, Marcus Tullius, 28, 70, 97, 134n28; *De oratore,* 23–24; *De senectute,* 124n19
Clément, Frère Jacques, 52, 67
Clermont, Collège de (Paris), 7
Coligny, Gaspard II de Châtillon, Sieur de, 6
colleges, Jesuit, 5, 11
Comuneros, 56, 69, 107
confessors, 9, 13, 84, 109
consolatio, 70, 128–29n1

Constance, Council of, 60, 68
constitutionalism, 51, 57, 61, 62, 105, 110, 111
Coton, Pierre, 67
courtiers, 55
Covarrubias, Diego de, 123n6, 125n22
crisis of monarchy, 44, 108–109
Crucifixion, date of, 93, 131n35
currency, 15, 16, 54, 59, 93, 109

dancing, 86, 87
deposition of monarchs, 58, 59, 60, 68
dialogues, 70, 81, 129n2
disorder, 55, 92, 104, 111
Divine Right, 67, 68, 110, 111
Dominican Order, 13

education, 9–10, 52, 61, 108, 111
elections, 48, 49, 53, 58
England, 15, 53, 105
ephoroi, 50, 58, 110
Erasmus, Desiderius, 52, 53, 65
Escorial, El, 11, 66
essay form, 78, 81, 111
exegesis, biblical, 5, 93

fables, 33–34, 41
falsos cronicones, 35–36, 119n50, 109
favorites, 50, 109, 110
Fernández de Velasco, Juan, Constable of Castile, 39, 82, 83
Fernando IV, King of Castile, 37
Fernando V, King of Spain (Ferdinand the Catholic), 26, 29, 43, 51, 58

flowers and gardening, 2, 47, 72, 73, 122n3
Fox Morcillo, Sebastián, 24
France, 5–7, 55, 66–68, 105, 108
Frederick II, King of Prussia, 111
freewill, 81, 90
Furió Ceriol, Fadrique, 53, 61, 62

Garibay, Esteban de, 24–25, 28, 34
Gellio, Agostino, 92
Gilimón de la Mota, Baltasar, 42, 120n68
Giovio, Paolo, Bishop of Nocera, 30
Golden Age topos, 122n4
Gómez Tejada, Cosme, 4
Góngora, Luis de, 102
Grace, 48, 76, 81
Gracián, Baltasar, 55
Granada, 8, 28, 29, 35, 82, 119n51
Gresham's Law, 15, 93–94
Guéret, Jean, 67
Guicciardini, Francesco, 43

harangues, 28, 29, 30, 31, 97, 98, 109
hedonism, 89
Henry III, King of Castile, 56, 94–95, 134n28
Henry IV, King of Castile, 29, 42, 43
Henry III, King of France, 6, 52, 66, 67
Henry IV, King of France, 6, 67
Herodotus, 33
hidalgos, 2
Hotman, François, 6

Huguenots, 5–6, 24
humor, 71
Hurtado de Mendoza, Juan, 3

Ignatius Loyola, St., 7, 11, 12, 71
Index expurgatorius, 10
Inquisition, 8, 17, 63, 70
irrigation, 54, 72, 73
Isabel the Catholic, Queen of Spain, 8, 29, 50
Isidore, St., Bishop of Seville, 14, 24, 28, 32, 34; Birthplaces and Death-Sites of the Saints, 83; Etymologies, 47, 59, 122n2, 123n8

James the Greater, St., Apostle, 36, 39, 129n9
James VI, King of Scotland (James I of England), 92
Jesuit Order, 7–13
Jews, 9, 21–22, 64, 114–15n48
Joan of Arc, St., 36
John of Salisbury, Bishop of Chartres, 121n89
Juan de Austria, Don, 13, 94
Juan de Mariana, oder die Entwickelungsgeschichte eines Jesuiten, 107
Justicia of Aragón (Lanuza, Juan de), 44, 50, 123n14
Justinian, Emperor, 57, 125n20

Knights Templar, 4, 36–37, 47

landscape, 47–48, 71–72, 75, 79–80, 100–102, 107, 132–33n16
Latin language, 9, 26, 52, 96, 98–100, 111

law and jurists, 44, 45, 51, 54, 56, 57, 62, 63, 109, 110, 124n21
leaden tablets, 35, 82, 119n50
legends, 24, 25, 34, 38, 109
Leonardo de Argensola, Bartolomé and Lupercio, 20, 27, 38, 87
Lerma, Francisco de Sandoval y Rojas, Duke of, 16, 17, 18, 86
limpieza de sangre, 62, 114n47
Lipsius, Justus, 127n42
Livy, 24, 29, 30, 31–32, 109
Llull, Ramon, 64
Loaisa, García de, Archbishop of Toledo, 4, 16, 47, 82, 86, 124n19
Locke, John, 105
López de Gómara, Francisco, 105
Luna, Álvaro de, 37, 43, 121n83
luxury, 66, 95

Machiavelli, Niccolò, 31, 43, 55, 65
Maimbourg, Louis, 20
Mallet du Pan, Jacques, 69
Mantuano, Pedro de Madrid, called Pedro, 38–42, 46, 82, 109, 120n73
Mariana, Juan de, humorlessness, 20: imprisonment, 17, 69, 95; misogyny, 3, 41; nationalism, 69; portrait, 19

WORKS
"Ad Castelionium in obitu uxoris et filiae" (To Castellonius on the Deaths of his Wife and Daughter), 102–104

"De adventu B. Iacobi Apostoli in Hispaniam" (On the Visit of St. James de Spain), 82–83
"De annis Arabum" (On the Islamic Calendar), 92
"De die mortis Christi" (On the Date of the Crucifixion), 92–93
"De monetae mutatione" (On Alterations in the Value of Currency), 17, 93–95
"De morte et immortalitate" (On Death and Immortality), 70–81, 111
De ponderibus et mensuris (On Weights and Measures), 92
De rege et regis institutione (On the King and his Training), 16, 47–69, 104–105, 107, 109, 110
"De spectaculis" (On Public Shows), 84–92, 111
"Densas sub salices" (hexameters), 100–102
Discurso de las enfermedades de la Compañía de Jesús (Discourse on the Errors in the Governance of the Society of Jesus), 10–13, 69
Historiae de rebus Hispaniae. Libri XXX (History of Spain in Thirty Books), 15
Historia general de España (General History of Spain), 3, 15, 26–30, 36–38, 40–41, 43–46, 105–106, 109–110
"Origen de los villanos que llaman cristianos viejos"

(Origin of the Peasants
Called Old Christians),
21–22, 114n47, 114n47
"Pro editione vulgata" (For the
Vulgate Edition of the
Bible), 93
"Respuesta" (Reply to Leonardo
de Argensola), 20, 27
*Scholia in Vetus et Novum
Testamentum* (Scholia to Both
Testaments), 93
Septem tractatus (Seven Treatises),
17, 95, 111
"Solivagum olim rudis"
(hexameters), 39–40
*Summarium ad Historiam
Hispaniae eorum quae acciderunt
annis sequentibus* (Summary of
Occurrences in the History of
Spain in Subsequent years),
43

Mariner, Vicente, 104
Martínez de Mariana, Juan, 2
Martínez de Toledo, Alfonso,
Archpriest of Talavera, 3
Martínez Guijeño, Juan (Siliceus),
Archbishop of Toledo, 4
Mayerne Turquet, Louis Turquet
de Mayerne, called, 24
maxims, 31, 44
Merlin, 37
Mézeray, François Eudes de,
33–34
Molina, Luis de, 81
monarchomachs, 61, 67, 123n14,
127n44
monarchy, 44, 69, 110

Mondéjar, Gaspar Ibáñez de
Segovia Peralta y Mendoza,
Marquis of, 46
Montaigne, Michel Eyquem, Sieur
de, 78
Morales, Ambrosio de, 25, 109
mozárabes, 21, 22
Munárriz, Josef Luis, 32, 46, 97,
106
music, 52

nature, 100, 102, 122n3, 122n6
New Christians, 21, 42
nobility, 6, 21, 39, 53, 54, 61,
62, 64, 108, 114n47
Novalis, Friedrich von
Hardenberg, called, 69
novels of chivalry, 41

Ocampo, Florián de, 24, 29, 34
Old Christians, 21, 62
origins, human, 48, 110, 122n4

papacy, 58, 65, 68
paradise, 79–81
Parlement of Paris, 68
parliamentarians, English, 105
Pasquier, Étienne, 36
patriotism, 22, 46, 69
Paul V, Pope, 68, 82
Pedro the Cruel, King of Castile,
37, 45, 121n83
people, 61–62, 64, 90, 111,
117n18, 131n28
Pérez, Antonio, 16, 108, 111,
123n14
Petrarch (Francesco Petrarca), 30,
43, 99–100
Philip II, King of Spain, 9, 11,
14, 15–16, 43, 50, 56,

60–61, 65, 77, 94, 108, 124n19, 125n26
Philip III, King of Spain, 16, 18, 47, 86, 108
Philip IV, King of Spain, 18
Philip IV, the Handsome, King of France, 37
Pi y Margall, Francisco, 106
Piélago, El, 4, 47–48
poison, 52, 60
Poland, 133n26
Politiques, 6, 67
Polybius, 32
poor, 54–55, 62–63
Portugal, 27, 43
predestination, 81
privados, 16, 108
profit-motive, 66, 91
prose style, 96–97, 106, 109–110, 111
providentialism, 28, 32, 37, 44, 51, 109, 121n88, 122n6
prudence, 44, 55, 63, 94, 116n5
psychic phenomena, 38
public administration, 52–53, 61, 62
Puebla Nueva, 3

Quintus Curtius, 33

Ranke, Leopold von, 105
Rapin, René, 106
Ratio studiorum, 9, 31, 111
Ravaillac, François, 66–67, 68, 110
rebellion, 58
Reconquista, 1, 8–9, 21, 22, 28, 66, 82, 109
regicide, 60, 68, 69, 104–105, 110

relics, 34–35, 129n10
resistance, 58, 60, 105
rhetoric, 116n5, 121n92
Rivadeneira, Pedro Ortiz de Cisneros, called Pedro de, 67, 86
Rodrigo, King of Spain, 29, 41
Rodrigo Jiménez de Rada, Archbishop of Toledo, 82
Rodríguez, Bernaldina, 2, 3, 14–15
Román de la Higuera, Jerónimo, 35
Rome, 5, 10, 35, 37
royalism, 60, 68, 69, 111
ruins, 122n3

Saavedra Fajardo, Diego de, *Corona gótica*, 126n35; *República literaria*, 97
Sago, Juan, 37
St. Bartholomew, Massacre of, 6
Salamanca, College at, 12
Salutati, Coluccio, 23, 120n60
Sánchez, Tomás, 87
Sánchez de las Brozas, Francisco (El Brocense), 104
Santa María, Collegiate Church of, 1, 3
sarabande, 86
secretaries, royal, 16, 108
secularization, 61, 106, 111
Sessa, Luis Fernández de Córdoba, Duke of, 18–19
Seyssel, Claude, 127–28n44
Sidney, Sir Philip, 33
Simancas, College at, 4
skittles, 74–75
Sobieski, Jakub, 17, 19
sociability, human, 58, 122n6

Sorbonne, College of La, 68
Soto, Francisco de, 1, 2
sources, historical, 32, 117n18
sports, 9, 73–75, 91
Stoicism, 79, 104, 116n5,
  127n42
Suárez, Francisco, 57–58, 60, 69
succession, monarchical, 49, 51,
  56, 58
syndications, 12, 63–64, 108

Tacitus, Publius Cornelius, 44,
  120n81
Talavera, 1–2, 15, 19, 112n5,
  113n13
Tamayo y Vargas, Tomás, 41–42,
  109
taxation, 51, 53, 54, 65–66
Thomas Aquinas, St., 57, 84
Toledo, 14, 15, 19, 29, 35–36,
  70, 71–72, 82, 104
toleration, religious, 55, 64, 111
Torrejón, Frey Andrés de, 1,
  113n13
trade and tariffs, 15, 16, 93
Turks, 22, 64
tyrannicide, 52, 59–60, 67–68,
  69, 104, 110

tyrants, 49, 51–52, 56, 57,
  59–61, 65, 67, 125n25

Urreta, Frey Luis de, 40
utopian writing, 13, 110

Vaca de Castro, Pedro,
  Archbishop of Granada, 35
vagabondage, 54, 55, 123n16
Valencia, Pedro de, 34, 41
validos, 16, 108
Vázquez de Menchaca, Fernando,
  122n6
Vega, Lope de, 42, 85, 89;
  Epistolario, 18–19;
  Fuenteovejuna, 104; *Triunfo de la
  fe en los reinos del Japón,* 18
vellón, 16, 94
Viperano, Giovanni, Bishop of
  Giovinazzo, 115–16n5
Virgil, 48, 98, 100, 102
Vitelleschi, Muzio, 6th. General
  of the Jesuits, 10
Vulgate edition of the Bible, 93

warfare, 29, 30, 44, 53–54, 63,
  65
witchcraft, 92

Zurita, Jerónimo de, 25, 28, 30,
  109